Self Coaching
Your Self-Mastery Road Map

Self Coaching Your Self-Mastery Road Map

Michael S. Haro, Ph.D.
and
Michael S. Haro, II, B.A.

Writer's Showcase
New York Lincoln Shanghai

Self Coaching Your Self-Mastery Road Map

All Rights Reserved © 2002 by Michael S. Haro, Ph.D.

No part of this book may be reproduced or transmitted in any form or by any means, graphic, electronic, or mechanical, including photocopying, recording, taping, or by any information storage retrieval system, without the written permission of the publisher.

Writer's Showcase
an imprint of iUniverse, Inc.

For information address:
iUniverse, Inc.
2021 Pine Lake Road, Suite 100
Lincoln, NE 68512
www.iuniverse.com

ISBN: 0-595-25747-X (pbk)

ISBN: 0-595-65305-7 (cloth)

Printed in the United States of America

To Lynne Y. Haro, wife and mother, for her unconditional love, support, encouragement, and guidance. She represents a standard and a pillar that stimulates excitement and excellence couched in confidence and the desire to succeed!
Thank you, Darling.
Thank you, Mom!

Contents

Foreword ix

Introduction 1

Chapter 1   Self Coaching: Your Self-Mastery Road Map 3

Chapter 2   Acquiring New Self Knowledge: Your Awareness Key 7

Chapter 3   Gaining Self Understanding: The Assessment Key 11

Chapter 4   Your Road Map: The Action Step 16

Chapter 5   Action Step #1: Understanding Yourself and the Power of Self-Control 23

Chapter 6   Action Step #2: Self-Image: Effectively Using Strengths and Limitations 30

Chapter 7   Action Step #3: Accept Responsibility and Accountability For Your Actions and Behaviors 40

Chapter 8   Action Step #4: Understand And Appreciate Your Talents And Commit to Their Maximum Use 50

Chapter 9   Action Step #5: Deal with Reality and Manage Uncertainty 60

Chapter 10   Action Step #6: Understand and Commit To Your Choices and Options 74

CHAPTER 11	Conclusion: Your New Beginning.	81
APPENDIX A	Affirmation Thoughts to Live By	85
APPENDIX B	Recommended Reading List	89
About the Authors		93
About the Center for Change Management		95

Foreword

By
John Weir, Ph.D.
Psychologist
San Rafael, CA

Anyone want to stay as they are? Certainly not!

Anyone want to change themselves? Oh yes!

We want to be healthier, eat better, lose weight, exercise, be more efficient, make more money, spend our money more wisely, be successful, get a promotion, be more effective, be kinder, be firmer, study more, work better, work smarter, work less, relax more, change careers, advance in our careers, retire from our career, be more serious, be more lighthearted, be more than we are, be all we can be. Whew!!!!!!! Some list. And if I had more time I could make it even longer.

How can we change ourselves? The ages-old questions. How can I release myself from my familiar limitations? How can I transform myself into the person I can so well imagine, but cannot seem to be?

In our primitive tribal past perhaps we sought greater reverence for the gods of the time in hope that personal change would be granted by the supernatural if we showed greater devotion. We looked to the priest, the elders, the shaman, for guidance on the actions that would result in a better life.

We still do. But now we look beyond belief and faith to knowledge and discovery. We ask that our experts and our science reveal the secret formula for personal change.

In the first half of the twentieth century many came to believe the engine of behavior lies buried deep in the unconsciousness of our earliest experience of infant and toddler life. We were the blank slate upon which the world wrote our destiny. Inconveniently, the most defining experiences hide in the shadows known only by their disguised appearance in dreams, fantasy, and the mysterious layering of everyday behavior.

Change could come from insight, an understanding of the emotional meaning of our behavior. With such insight, we might transfer some control of our life from the unconscious to the conscious, from the irrational to the rational. Applying the method of insight and emotional discovery does result in self-change, but it doesn't work on everything and it doesn't work for everybody.

In the middle of the century some proposed we shift our focus and our efforts to other science and other experts. They showed us that the direction of effect is not only from emotions to thought and behavior, but also from thought and behavior to emotion. They proposed we analyze our thinking and our actions to generate the capacity for successful self-change. This idea became a foundation for what are known generally as the cognitive-behavioral theories of human experience. Cognitive-behavioral theories are the basis for methods of personal change through self-directed applications of theoretical principles.

This book on self-mastery is the latest example of how cognitive-behavioral methods for personal change can be applied for success in your life. Follow the process of Awareness, Assessment, and Action proposed by the authors to gain new self-mastery. Discover within this book your path to self-change through knowledge, understanding, and behavior.

Introduction

o o o o o o o o o o o o o o o o o o o o o o o o o o o o o
"Only those who risk going too far can possibly find out how far one can go."

—*T.S. Eliot*

Self Coaching is a learned process. Using it helps individuals gather facts regarding situations or events in which they are involved, learn how to center these facts in the here-and-now, and then determine what can be done right now to influence productive outcomes.

The Self Coaching (Self-Mastery) Model is built on three phases:

AWARENESS	(WHY?)	Information Processing
ASSESSMENT	(HOW?)	Understanding
ACTION	(WHAT?)	Commitment, Direction, Implementation, and Results

Read this book and you will begin to raise your level of awareness. Ask, "Why are things happening to me the way they are?" Start generating information and facts surrounding what you're doing, then move to the assessment phase. Here you can generate an understanding that will allow you to develop a plan of action, a direction. With your plan of action, you can generate actions and behaviors necessary to carry you forward. Evaluate your results. Make necessary adjustments, and always put yourself in a position to continue to be productive. Do what you can do, and do it now!

KEY LEARNING FACTOR #1

SELF-MASTERY MODEL FOR MODIFYING BEHAVIOR

AWARENESS (The "WHY")

- Information, facts, opinions, myths
- Attitudes, Beliefs, Things that are real or possible

ASSESSMENT (The "HOW")

- Understanding needs, goals, expectations
- Direction and Plan of Action

Action (The "WHAT")

- Application
- Wisdom of action and commitment

1

Self Coaching: Your Self-Mastery Road Map

o o o o o o o o o o o o o o o o o o o o o o o o o o o o o
"What lies behind us and what lies before us are tiny matters, compared to what lies within us."

—**Ralph Waldo Emerson**

In troubling times it's not uncommon to find yourself struggling with the concept of success. What are these times of trouble? Try these on for size: Businesses, large and small, are failing. Poor management and greed are leaving loyal employees with no retirement, no jobs, and not much hope for the future. The Wall Street Journal reported that the scope of corporate transgressions is greater than anything Americans have experienced since the years before the Great Depression. Surveys indicate that optimism about the economy is weak. Is it fair to say that your will to succeed is being challenged?

Welcome to ***Self Coaching: Your Self-Mastery Road Map***. By using this book as a road map or guide, you've selected a tool to help you expand your options. Through new knowledge you have an opportunity to identify alternate roadways, discover new possibilities, and venture in directions that may lead to new and exciting adventures.

Your past experiences likely have included negative barriers and roadblocks. You may have experienced failures. But placed in the context of this book, you now will have the tools to begin turning these negative experiences into stepping stones that can lead to improved performances and successes.

Life experiences are filled with stress and conflict. Many of these conflicts create *dis*tress, a negative and unproductive form of stress. Your ability to cope with such experiences is dependent on the information received, the way you perceive it, the importance it's given, and how you're influenced by it. Turning a negative into a positive is a self coaching tool that will come in handy for you.

Self Coaching is a process by which you can begin to do a reality check on yourself. Here are a few questions to get you thinking at a self coaching level.

- **Are you satisfied with what you're doing?**
- **Are you where you want to be?**
- **Do you get frustrated and angry?**
- **Do you get down on yourself when you make a mistake?**
- **Do you feel guilty because others seem disappointed in you?**
- **Are you unhappy with many of your life decisions?**
- **Do you spend a lot of time wishing things were different?**

Answering questions like these opens the road map and places the "you are here" star on the point where you find yourself right now. Your actions or inactions, decisions or indecisions, choices or acceptances are going to lead you to the next level—positively or negatively. Your road map opened when you started reading this book. So let's start your journey.

When you think that you cannot change a situation, it's time to recognize that your perception is faulty. Carrying the burden of false perception is to live a life of desperation. You can recognize distress by tuning into your mood or disposition. If you're feeling worried, nervous, overly excited, and insecure, you're probably showing signs of distress. You will learn to reevaluate your situation by using the techniques taught in *Self Coaching: Your Self-Mastery Road Map*.

This book will help you develop an understanding of yourself and others, and create an inner balance. By using the information presented in the following chapters, you'll be provided with success oriented tools. You'll be able to raise your level of awareness and take direct control of your decisions. Your search will center on self-confidence, self-respect, self-satisfaction and self-development. When balance is achieved in these areas, a well-adjusted and fulfilled life becomes a viable option.

Self-Mastery is a power within that enables you to make critical choices, and to give meaning and commitment to these choices. It aids in the initial tasks of building, living within, and continually producing a positive life structure. The self coaching self-mastery process is a road map and guidance tool. If used correctly, it will help you establish destinations as you continue your journey through life.

KEY LEARNING FACTOR #2

AS YOU THINK, SO YOU GO!!

**Your thinking directs
   Your actions and behaviors
      That gets you your results**

2

Acquiring New Self Knowledge: Your Awareness Key

o o o o o o o o o o o o o o o o o o o o o o o o o o o o
*"Ask a question and you're a fool for three minutes;
do not ask a question and you're a fool the rest of your life."*

—**Chinese Proverb**

Everything that you need to improve your productivity can be found within you. *Self Coaching: Your Self-Mastery Road Map* will hand you the keys and your road map. The rest is up to you.

It is now time to hand you the keys. The first key is awareness.

> **AWARENESS**
> *The knowledge and facts needed for self-mastery. This information is sometimes based on opinions and myths.*
>
> **Beliefs**
> *Real or possible*
>
> **"Who am I?"**
>
> I am important.
> I am unique.
> "I am OK!"

Figure 1: An outline of the Self-Mastery Awareness Step

7

If you're a dreamer and can come up with creative ideas, you're ready for the **"Awareness Key."** This key is the first step in your reality check. Don't forget that being a dreamer is a positive attribute. Most great accomplishments start with dreams. Dreamers who are willing to work make those dreams a reality. The will to work is the driving force.

Using the *Awareness Key* challenges you to think. Your dreams may have been a great motivator but now you must begin the task of changing your dreams into a reality. Reality begins with sound facts and accurate information. You need to determine what is real or possible for you to manage productively.

As you begin to use the *Awareness Key*, the knowledge base becomes exposed. How do you see yourself? Your self-esteem is a key indicator and provides substantial data as to how you're currently functioning or wish to be functioning. Ask the question, "Who am I?" Two immediate, distinct, and direct answers are provided for this question: You are unique, and you are important. You're unique because there is only one of you in the whole world. No one can ever take that away from you. No matter how hard they try, they cannot take away your uniqueness. You can't even give it away. This is an indisputable fact.

Secondly: You are important. This is true until you turn over your importance or give it away. You might say: "What I did is really stupid. I am stupid." Listen to what you're saying. Can you see how you're giving away your importance through the second statement? In reality you're still important. The action you took or behavior demonstrated may not have been appropriate, but you're still able to think, reflect and process. Therefore, you're not stupid, and you still have importance. Remember, regardless of what's happening to you or around you, as long as you can believe that you're OK, you can maintain control. You might make a big mistake, but you can still be OK. Your actions and behaviors temporarily might be inappropriate, but if you can focus on being OK, you have the option of turning this negative into something positive. If you dwell on the negative and beat yourself about the head and neck, you'll have nothing to build on. Stop the negative. Make a positive statement. Admit that what you did was inappropriate or even wrong. It may have been totally unproductive. However, you're still OK if you can generate alternatives. Through your positive thinking, you can adjust your actions and behaviors. It is your thinking that guides your actions and behaviors, and these produce your results.

Wisdom is derived by learning from your experiences, not from the punishment you inflict on yourself. Stop. Don't repeat unproductive behaviors. Think OK thoughts. Generate OK actions and behaviors. Remind yourself to do everything within your power not to repeat the negative behaviors. Through this type of thinking you take control and you become more productive.

Now you are at a point where, regardless of what's going on, you can say that you're OK. You must take this position if you're going to succeed and move ahead. When you do this, when you can say that you are OK and truly believe it, then you're ready for the next key.

Five Steps To Achieving the Awareness Key

1. **Stop the negative.**
2. **Make a positive statement (I am unique; I am important).**
3. **Do everything in your power not to repeat the negative action.**
4. **Recognize that you are okay.**
5. **Take control and be productive.**

KEY LEARNING FACTOR #3

The Power of Positive Thinking

I'm OK!	I'm Not OK!
'OK' Thinking	Not 'OK' Thinking
Leads to	Leads to
Positive Actions	Negative Actions

Positive thinking allows you to adjust your actions and behaviors.

3

Gaining Self Understanding: The Assessment Key

o o o o o o o o o o o o o o o o o o o o o o o o o o o o o
*"Tell them and they will forget;
Show them and they will remember;
Involve them and they will learn."*

—**Chinese Proverb**

The **Assessment Key** allows you to look at your needs, goals, and expectations.

ASSESSMENT
*Your needs, goals, and expectations
as related to the factual
information regarding one's
strengths and weaknesses.*

Attitudes
*Your Plan of Action
Direction*

"What am I?"

I'm capable.

Figure 2: An outline of the Self-Mastery Assessment Step

Everyone has needs and expectations. You're where you are right now because you've been attempting to satisfy your needs. Whatever's happening to you right now is an attempt to satisfy a need or an expectation. Were you conscious of the desire to pick up this book and to read? Did you clearly establish a goal—what you hoped to accomplish by reading this book? It is very unlikely that you took the time to go through such an exercise. You likely were operating in an automatic level of thinking, but were motivated by something. Perhaps an expectation to learn something new, a need to relax for a few minutes, or to try to change direction temporarily. Regardless, you were motivated by an inner drive, conscious or subconscious.

Think about self-mastery for a moment. The power within allows you to start taking mastery over bits and pieces of your actions and behaviors. Automatic or conscious thinking directs our activities. You can achieve self-mastery automatically or with conscious thought by engaging the assessment phase of the model. You attain mastery with the automatic level of thinking when you practice achieving your needs, goals, or expectations through repetitive behaviors. You can adjust those behaviors by becoming conscious of the actions that are not producing the results you desire. At the conscious level of thinking, you can select options and make adjustments in your actions and behaviors to obtain the desired results.

The *assessment* process helps you to look at the question: "What do I really need?" Obtaining a level of mastery through assessment puts you in a position where you can select more productive action steps for accomplishing your goals. When you have gathered and know the facts, develop your needs based on what's real and possible. Your belief in yourself will become stronger. You're developing a strength that brings confidence to your ability to make positive and productive decisions in every aspect of your life. This is reflected in your attitude.

Attitude reflects your needs and your goals through the actions and behaviors you demonstrate. Interestingly enough, everyone has an attitude. When you see or observe another person, you see their attitude.

When they look at you, they see your attitude. What do they see? Do they see a smile or a frown? Do they see excitement or despair, enjoyment or sadness, expectation or desperation? What do they see? In reality they see your attitude. Attitude is your manifested behavior, what you show to others through your actions. It's behavior that's with you at all times. Have you ever noticed how some people have such a great attitude? These are the people who can walk *into* a room and light it up. Then there are those people who have such an attitude that when they walk *out* of a room, it lights up.

What attitudes do you show? How are you demonstrating your needs and goals to others, and to yourself? Remember what others see is a perception of what they believe you're feeling or thinking. This is their reality. To take control, be aware of the actions and behaviors you are presenting to others. Positive thinking produces positive actions and demonstrates to others a positive attitude. Negative thinking reverses this process and produces the opposite results. Which do you want to be casting?

Look at what you're feeling, what you believe to be real or possible. This is based on your awareness, the information you have about a situation and about yourself. What do you believe is happening? Are you in control? Can you regain control? Believe in yourself. Remember: You're unique. You're important. Start telling yourself these things. Believe them.

You can demonstrate positive behavior if you're generating positive thoughts. Others will see these results as well. Practicing positive thinking is a skill that can be learned, and is a productive way of taking care of yourself. Realistically, if you're taking good care of yourself, you're in a much better position to assist others. Keep a good handle on your awareness issues. Stand guard at the doorway to your mind. Be aware of how your thoughts are directing your actions and behaviors. Be conscious of your needs, goals, and expectations when you enter an important activity. Understand that you're capable of performing whatever you believe to be real or possible.

You can begin to build when you know your capabilities. This understanding is based on the fact that you're maintaining an OK position even though the situation isn't where you might like it to be. You can always do things that are productive for you. Be thinking at the conscious level. Try out your options. Continuously adjust those factors that block your progress. You can do this because you're electing to take control of *your* actions and behaviors. You can't control anyone else's behaviors, but you can control yours. By reminding yourself, by saying "I'm OK," "I'm Capable," you're ready to take the third step in the process of Self-Mastery. You're ready for **Action**.

KEY LEARNING FACTOR #4

| *Self-Mastery* | and the | *Chinese Proverb* |

- **<u>AWARENESS:</u>**　　　　　　　　　　*<u>Tell Them</u>*

  Help answer the "Why?" with information and facts.

- **<u>ASSESSMENT:</u>**　　　　　　　　　*<u>Show Them</u>*

  Use the information and facts to show "How" this fits needs, goals, and expectations.

- **<u>ACTION:</u>**　　　　　　　　　　　　*<u>Involve them</u>*

  Taking the information from the "Why" and the processing from "How," discuss the steps to get "What" actions and behaviors.

Measure your results and reuse the process as needed.

4

Your Road Map: The Action Step

> *"The credit belongs to the man who is actually in the arena, whose face is marred by dust and sweat and blood...who knows the great enthusiasms, the great devotions, who spends himself in a worthy cause; who at the best knows in the end the triumph of high achievement, and...if he fails, at least fails while daring greatly, so that his place shall never be with those cold and timid souls who know neither victory or defeat."*
>
> —*Theodore Roosevelt*

It is now time for you to receive your road map. The actions to be taken are determined in part by your awareness and assessment. Having collected the information, assessed your situation, and developed a plan of action, you're ready for the challenge. The direction is set. You must now put yourself in motion, start taking action.

Let's compare your action steps to those of taking a trip and putting a car in motion. Interestingly enough, once you get in the car, map in hand, destination in mind, and the capability of achieving the end result, you still must take command and control to make this event happen. Even though you have a very reliable vehicle, in good running order, well maintained, and fueled for the journey, you still must take charge in the driver's seat.

If you get in the car and say, "OK, I'm ready to go. Go car. Go," nothing will happen. Nothing happens until you make a decision to take action. So you put the key in the ignition, and start the car. Once again, you say "Go car. Go." The engine is running, the scene is set, but nothing happens. Even with the best-laid plan, information all in order, needs and goals determined, the vehicle powered up and ready to go, *you still need to take control.*

How? First, put the car in gear. Next, take hold of the steering wheel. Now manage the gas and break pedals. You're ready for **Action.**

Action
This is your ability to take factual information and incorporate it into a personal needs/goals base. Your actions will allow you to direct yourself and commit to your productivity.

Commitments
Values

"What do you want to do?"

You can be whatever you believe is real or possible and whatever you believe you're capable of being.

Figure 3: An outline of the Self-Mastery Action Step

The six chapters that follow discuss action steps that can facilitate self coaching and help you develop the self-mastery process. Using these steps and the suggestions offered, you can begin to match your awareness (knowledge) and assessment (understanding) factors and start to achieve the actions and outcomes desired. The six action steps are:

1) Understanding Yourself and the Power of Self-Control

Achievement and happiness are two attainable goals. Achievement is the result of your actions and behaviors. Happiness is the state of mind that supports the thought processes that help drive you to achieve your outcomes. Success levels will differ based on the way you plan, organize, and take control of your productivity. If you're not achieving the level of success you desire, you are probably letting other people or situations take control. If you are blaming others for your bad breaks, underestimating your potential, giving in to fear instead of conquering it, failing to set clear goals, and thinking defeat instead of victory, then you're on the wrong road. Open your road map. Read it because you're going the wrong way. This chapter will help you locate yourself. It will stop you from continuing down a dead end street.

2) Self-Image: Effectively Using Your Strengths and Limitations

A major contributor to human personality and human behavior is your self-image. Your self-image assists you in setting boundaries and guiding you toward successful outcomes. An adequate, realistic self-image will help you to expand your possibilities. With the power of a positive self-image you can develop new capabilities, new talents—pathways that can literally turn failure into success. This chapter will help you identify your strengths and limitations.

3) Accept Responsibility and Accountability for Your Actions and Behaviors

Success in self-mastery is not accidental. It is not something that you simply can wish to happen. You are responsible for your success. You make it happen. You can produce outstanding results by doing specific activities to create those results. The pathway to excellence will be paved with the results you're willing to pay for with hard work, time, and all out effort. To produce the results you desire, you must be willing to take actions that will create your desired outcomes. This chapter will help you identify control factors for directing your efforts.

4) Understand and Appreciate Your Talents and Commit to Their Maximum Use

By knowing your unique strengths, and committing to their productive use, you'll always be more capable of adapting to changing circumstances. You can take control of the things that you are aware of. You can develop a plan of action to understand them more completely. You'll always be presented with many forks in the road. At each of these forks, you'll have the freedom and the power to choose. The choices you make, the manner in which you respond, will determine the eventual outcomes. Prepare yourself and be ready to deal with these decision opportunities. This chapter will prepare you to commit to your strengths and rely on them for your energy.

5) Deal With Reality and Manage Uncertainty

Self-mastery is a road map that can help you negotiate the highways of life. If the road map is accurate, you'll generally know where you are and how you got there. More importantly, if you decide to go somewhere you've never been, you'll have a guide to help you get there. If you find yourself confused or lost, check to see if the road map is outdated or inaccurate.

Since you weren't born with a road map, you will have to make your own. It involves effort and experience. It comes from your relationships with others and your self-directed thoughts. You'll produce a larger and more accurate road map as you learn to appreciate and perceive reality. This is accomplished by checking your information to make sure it is real and possible. Then you apply that understanding by putting together realistic plans of action. These plans are achieved using your abilities and capabilities.

To keep your maps accurate, you must evaluate and revise them continually. You can do this by exploring options and the mystery of reality. It's your decision to take control or to be controlled. You're always in a position to expand, refine, or redefine your understanding of the world in which you live. A tough, yet important lesson to learn is when to seek or ask for help. If your road map isn't guiding you and you're in need of revising it, you're due for some assistance. Present and expose your reality map to the criticism and challenge of other map makers. This process can be difficult. Confronting and problem solving can be painful. It's this very process, however, through which you will learn to grow and develop. This chapter refocuses on this growth process.

6) Understand and Commit to Your Choices and Options

"Constructive coping" is a process of confronting tasks and developing appropriate responses. Through this process you can learn how to adequately deal with difficult tasks or decisions. The goal of constructive coping is to help you make the type of decisions that will put you in a place where you can continue to be productive. This chapter helps you recognize your coping behaviors and suggests ways of putting them to productive use.

<u>*Your Road Map*</u>

To effectively use the Self—Mastery Road Map, follow this guideline.

<u>***Awareness:***</u> The question associated with Awareness is *Why?* Anytime you're asking yourself "*Why?*" or you hear someone else asking "*Why?*" more information is needed. Information is often bound in factual knowledge, opinion, or myth. Regardless of the source, work to get the facts as best can be determined. Try to eliminate the emotional influences or content. Once the facts are established you can keep the emotional influence to a minimum by asking yourself, "What can I do right now?" This keeps you centered in the here-and-now. By taking these facts, you can start…

Assessment: The question associated with Assessment is "*HOW?*" Asking "*How?*" implies a need for more understanding of the situation. "How did this happen?" "How can I start moving forward?" "How" helps take the information from the Awareness and starts constructing a plan of action. Resist the temptation to jump to action because it's likely you're not ready. Think about how you've handled situations like this in the past. Review actions and behaviors you've taken, assess how effective they have been for you. Keep the actions and behaviors that worked, and make adjustments to those that didn't. Also, be creative with options that might be new but likely will work. Ask, "How can I approach this situation with the information and the new strategies I have identified?" This provides you with a direction and plan of action. It helps you identify your needs and goals. This also provides a foundation for control. Now you're ready for…

Action: The question associated with Action is "*WHAT?*" "What do I do now?" Your "*What*" question implies a need for direction. You support this direction with the information from Awareness and the understanding from Assessment. Look at what you can do right now, fold that into your plan of action, and start implementing the actions and behaviors that you believe will help you take control of the situation. Control implies a form of management that will allow you to continue to be productive and move forward. Once you've taken your actions, evaluate the results coming from these actions. All actions and behaviors produce measurable results. As you look at your results, determine their effectiveness in helping you manage the situation. If something isn't helping, take that specific behavior or action back through the model—Awareness, Assessment, and Action. Ask, "Do I need to adjust my information?" "Do I need to revise my plan of action?" and "What adjustments do I need to make to my plan?"

This is your road map. Remember it is only a guide and needs your direct involvement to make it work.

KEY LEARNING FACTOR #5

Problem Solving Approach

AWARENESS: Fact/Knowledge

Resolving a Problem: Arriving at a decision or conclusion that everybody is completely satisfied with and ready to move forward.

Managing a Problem: Arriving at a decision or conclusion that allows you to continue to be productive and positive about your efforts.

ASSESSMENT: Needs/Goals/Expectations

How can you best manage a challenge or problem? Remember:
You always have options and choices.
Be prepared to deal with decision opportunities.
Learn to manage the situation; don't let it manage you.

ACTION: Deciding what you can do.

Take control. Make a decision to act based on the facts (Awareness) and a well thought out plan of action (Assessment).
Review your results. If productive, continue.
If unproductive, check your facts and your understanding of the situation or event.

5

Action Step #1: Understanding Yourself and the Power of Self-Control

"A habit cannot be tossed out of the window. It must be coaxed down the stairs, a step at a time."

—*Mark Twain*

Your will to succeed will be reinforced when you examine the information you're receiving and examine how your needs, goals, and expectations are impacted. Challenges are a given in this rapidly changing society. Facing those things you fear the most starts with your ability to determine whether you're reacting or responding to the event or situation. **Reacting** is emotionally driven, while **responding** is thinking and processing rationally. Your response to fear is determined by what you're thinking about as it pertains to the situation as opposed to the situation itself. To truly gain control and manage a situation, you must first be able to accurately interpret the event or situation. Secondly, you must develop a level of understanding by giving it meaning. Once interpreted, and meaning attached, you can determine its value to you. At this point you're in a position to start worrying, or to take control. Healthy fear can stimulate and alert you to dangers that are real. Your will to succeed remains intact. You're responding and operating out of the intellectual center. You're starting to manage the challenge. If you start reacting, you're operating out of the emotional center. Irrational or inappropriate fear takes over and leads to under-productive behavior, often delaying or subverting your ability to manage or stay in control.

Here are some ways to effectively understand and manage your challenges:

Establish Your Goals by Focusing And Setting Boundaries

Expectations for the future provide opportunities and new challenges. Needs and goals begin to emerge followed by the desire to satisfy and reach them. Preparing to meet these challenges and striving to reach new goals will be no different than experiences you've already faced. Your activities up to this point have been guided and directed by rules and regulations. Standards and guidelines were established to lead and guide you to goal, need, or expectation related events such as participation in family, school, and social activities, graduation from high school or college, and established careers or jobs. Reaching your next level of success could well depend on your ability to set your own boundaries and to learn to stay within those boundaries.

Let's explore career decision making. Ask yourself, "Am I satisfied with the progress I'm making in my career?" If you can truthfully answer yes to this question, then you're within your boundaries. You're successfully meeting your daily challenges. This isn't to say that you're without problems. But you're able to turn problems into challenges. These challenges are obviously controlled within your ability range. This allows you to stay satisfied, stimulated, or encouraged by what you're doing.

What about those of us who are not satisfied with what's going on in our work lives? There are people who are not satisfied and feel like prisoners of work. Their 9:00 to 5:00 jobs have become a sentence that locks them up on a daily basis. Why is there such unhappiness?

If this last paragraph fits you, you're not a happy camper. Unfortunately with this level of unhappiness, you're likely to be displaying a negative attitude. This attitude comes from your thinking, and others are observing your actions and behaviors. Your negative thinking perpetuates itself because you're constantly reminding yourself of:

—things you can't do,

—things you should've done, or

—things you wish you would've done.

A negative attitude is a product of your thinking. This type of thinking translates into negative choices, actions, and behaviors. All actions and behaviors are driven by how you're thinking. The results you get come from your actions and behaviors. This explains how you perpetuate the negatives and live in a state of unhappiness.

It's your choice and decision to continue in this unhappy direction. If you are negative, you made a choice to be negative. Your actions and behaviors are putting your choices in motion. Have you taken conscious control of these decisions? Are you setting your own boundaries, or have you allowed them to be set for you? What is it that you want to do? What changes are you willing to make? These are the questions you need to start asking yourself. Stop focusing on how unhappy you are at this time. Become aware of the decisions you are making to direct things in your life. Think about this statement: "You're right now exactly what you want to be." If you desire to change, start by setting new boundaries.

Life is like a puzzle. When its pieces are all in the box, it can look like an impossible task to complete. But like the puzzle, life can be an exciting challenge. All the pieces are there. All you have to do is go to work and put the pieces together.

If you're having challenges with happiness and satisfaction, whether it be related to work, family, social, or self, go after these challenges by setting boundaries. First, try to see the challenge as a jigsaw puzzle. It may be a 1,000-pieces or a 5,000-pieces puzzle. The interesting thing about a puzzle is that you usually have an idea of what the completed project will look like. You can create an outcome scenario for your challenge if you're willing to set a goal or result that you want to achieve.

Here are the steps. When starting to put a puzzle together most people look for the straight edges or corner pieces. Ask yourself why this logic, and you immediately realize that by selecting these pieces first, you automatically start working on the boundaries of the puzzle.

Once boundaries are set and you start organizing, you can build the puzzle area by area. As long as you stay within the boundaries, you can work on different areas and still make progress. This also is true for the puzzles of life. You don't have to stay in one place until you find the next piece that lets you go forward. You might get stuck in your career, a job, or a personal relationship because you don't explore other areas within your boundaries. You might lack creative actions, get bored, frustrated, or disillusioned. Before you know it, you're focused on the negatives and reacting with unproductive or underproductive behaviors.

Believing that you can't move forward can lock you in. You might become blocked because of being denied a promotion or get rejected in a relationship. Regarding the promotion, you start thinking that you should've made a different decision out of high school or college. Thinking in the past has a debilitating effect on you. There is nothing you can do about your past decisions except learn from them. They've been made. Refocus and ask "What can I do right now?" Maintain your boundaries and explore how you can maximize your effort with the current situation. Don't overreact, stay in bounds and make adjustments that will help you move forward. As for the relationship and rejection, become aware of what you're thinking. If you feel that you are unable to progress without this other person, you've become a prisoner in your own mind. You're trapped by an unwillingness to explore other sections of your puzzle. By fixating on the rejected relationship, you've done nothing to reach out to other viable or growth producing relationships. Your vision has been limited and you've stopped exploring your options. You've turned control over to the situation or person that produced the negative, and you're perpetuating it. Stop, and become creative. Never stop looking for options. This is what keeps you productive.

Master Exercise:

Using your Self-Mastery Road Map, complete the following exercise.
Awareness: "Why am I…(happy, unhappy, satisfied, or dissatisfied) with the event or situation I am facing today?" Spell out the facts that are involved with the situation or event. Be specific and stay out of the emotional state. Do this by using "I" statements such as "I'm not taking control because I have not done…"
Assessment: "How can I begin to change or adjust this situation or event in a way that will allow me to be more productive or advance?" Look at the facts in Awareness. Pick out one that you feel is important and think you can do something with at this time. Ask the question above. Be specific and lay out a plan of action or direction that'll move you toward your goal or expectation.
Action: "What can I do right now to implement my plan of action or new direction?" Taking the plan of action developed in Assessment and keeping in mind the information you're coping with in Awareness, start taking the actions and behaviors that'll move you forward. Actions will produce results. These are the measurable factors that indicate your level of success. If you're not getting the results you want, take that fact and run it through your road map. If you're getting productive results, keep doing what you're doing because it is working.

Self-Control: A Way To Enhance Your Life

Self-Control is a skill based thought process that can guide your actions and behaviors and produce positive results. Disciplining yourself to sit down and write out what you think might be done to adjust current behaviors is part of this process. By raising your awareness level to expand knowledge, the assessment level can work to provide a foundation for understanding. With knowledge and understanding in place, the motivation and drive to take steps to create new directions is enhanced. Practicing these sequences helps you focus and maintain productivity.

Self-control can be useful in establishing goals and expectations. The following five points can help to develop and reinforce self-control skills.

1. Work to develop strong motivation, a desire to succeed. Motivation is internal and is based on your thinking. Be active and positive with your thoughts. Your thinking directs your actions and behaviors that get you your results.

2. Be aware of what it is you wish to accomplish. Write it down. Writing raises your level of awareness to a conscious, focused position. Once at this level, you're one step away from the creative level of thinking—the options arena.

3. Use relaxation to minimize stress and concentrate deeply during periods of meditation. Distress lowers your ability to be productive. Relaxation lowers your stress levels and increases your ability to be productive.

4. Know how to use your imagination in a creative manner. Creativity opens you to an options arena. This is a virtual buffet of thinking. The more you open the buffet, the more options you have available.

5. Become a positive thinker, and apply visualization to find solutions. Remember, "As you think, so you go." Your thinking directs your actions and behaviors that get you your results. Positive thinking will help produce positive and productive results in your life.

Action Step #1: Understanding Yourself and the Power of Self-Control   29

KEY LEARNING FACTOR #6

THOUGHT GENERATORS

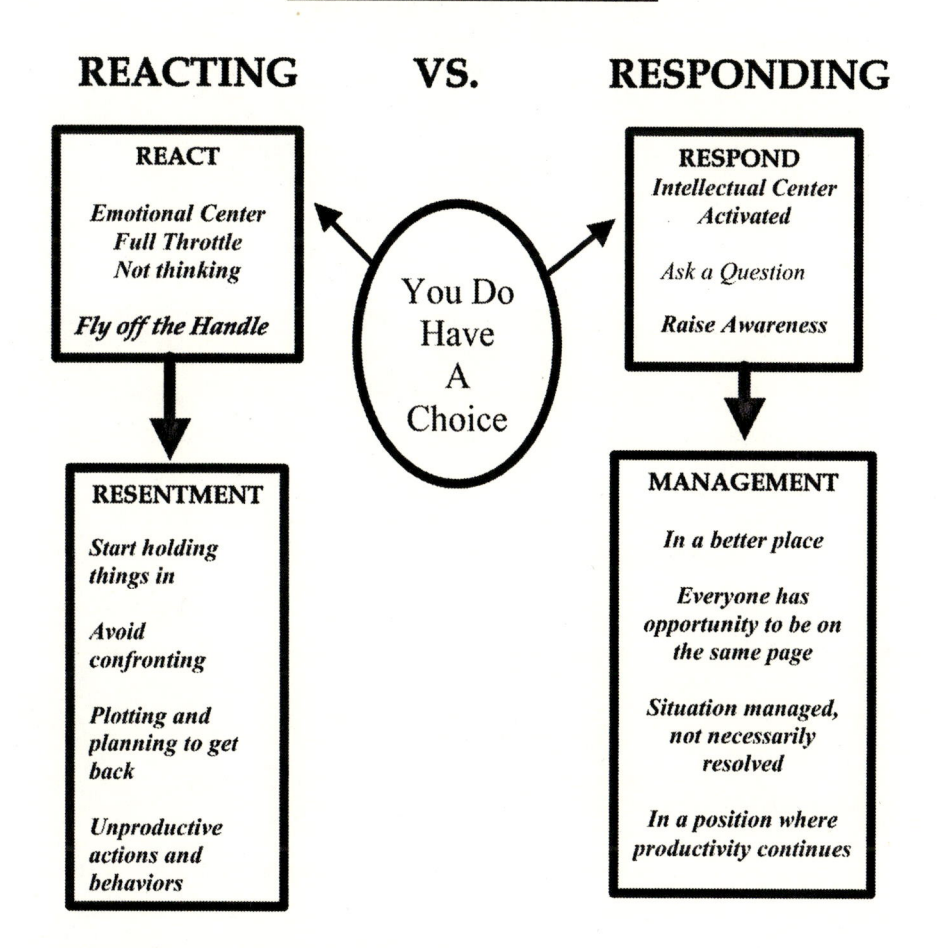

REACTING   VS.   **RESPONDING**

REACT

*Emotional Center
Full Throttle
Not thinking*

Fly off the Handle

RESPOND
*Intellectual Center
Activated*

Ask a Question

Raise Awareness

You Do Have A Choice

RESENTMENT

Start holding things in

Avoid confronting

Plotting and planning to get back

Unproductive actions and behaviors

MANAGEMENT

In a better place

Everyone has opportunity to be on the same page

Situation managed, not necessarily resolved

In a position where productivity continues

Reacting is emotionally driven.
Irrational thought or inappropriate fear takes over.

Responding is intellectually driven.
Options are available and you decide your direction.

6

Action Step #2: Self-Image: Effectively Using Strengths and Limitations

"I've never met a person, I don't care what his condition, in whom I could not see possibilities. I don't care how much a man may consider himself a failure, I believe in him, for he can change the thing that is wrong in his life at any time he is ready and prepared to do it. Whenever he develops the desire, he can take from his life the thing that is defeating it. The capacity for reformation and change lies within."

—**Preston Bradley**

Flip the Coin

Do you go through life evaluating your every move? Are you constantly reminding yourself of the things you can't do, should have done, or wish you would've done? How many times have you said to yourself, "I just can't lose that weight I gained over the holidays?" Listen to the message you're giving yourself. Could it be that you don't really want to lose the weight, but are wishing for a miracle?

In reality, you are where you're ready to be. If you argue, "no this is not where I want to be" then restate your self-talk message. For example, "I can lose the weight I gained over the holidays. I just haven't motivated myself to the point of getting it done." This is where you are, and where you've chosen to be based on your behaviors. There is hope. You don't have to beat yourself up or go into a state of depression. Just flip the coin.

Flipping the coin is a way of focusing on the positive side of the situation and giving yourself the support you need to handle challenges that arise on a daily basis. By flipping the coin, you can take control of a situation and approach it more logically and rationally. When you become aware of a negative, flip the coin. See what the positive side looks like. Now, start thinking about this positive side and how you can make adjustments to bring about the more productive results. Make a decision and regain control of the situation or event.

Remember this: "All negatives have a positive side. Likewise, all positives have a negative side." The coin can land on either side. "I can't seem to do anything right," is the negative side of the coin. Flip again, or turn the coin over, and you have: "There are many things I can do right. Right now, I'm making a mistake by acting this way." The question becomes, "Do I want to continue making this mistake?" If not, then consider your options.

Learn to become your own best friend. Give yourself a chance to experience life on the flip side if the current side isn't providing the positive and rewarding components to "being where you want to be." By raising your level of awareness, and thinking the opposite of the negative that's currently controlling you, you become more logical and rational. You also have just increased you ability to get back in control.

EXERCISE:

Are you currently confronting a negative situation or event? If so, take that situation or event and try "flipping the coin." Specifically state the negative that you are experiencing. Now, flip that statement and write it out as a positive statement. Run this positive statement through the "Master Exercise."

Managing Your Tough Times

"Tough times never last, but tough people do" is a slogan proposed by Dr. Robert Schuller. Yes, you've faced tough times. A tough time may have involved that very first love. When things didn't work out, you thought the world would come to an end. It didn't, and that tough time passed. There was a lesson in that experience. It taught you that interpersonal relationships can be difficult, and that if you invest in relationships, you can get hurt emotionally. That learning experience didn't stop you from reinvesting in relationships. Rather, by learning about yourself and others, you were in a better position to operate more effectively in your next relationship.

You'll have the opportunity to experience many tough situations. There'll be information available on what to do or not to do. You may or may not make the best use of the situation or information. In fact, you may have to make several runs through these tough times before finally making the right choices to have things work out. These experiences and your ability to manage them is your confirmation that "tough people do last!"

You have personality traits that can lead you through tough or difficult times. Personality traits also can be responsible for holding you back or pulling you down. Knowing about your personality strengths and limitations can be invaluable for leading you through tough times.

Let's examine your "personality armor." The way you think about a challenge and process it provides you with information about your abilities to cope. Remember, your thinking or lack of thinking directs your actions and behaviors. How you handle anger, face problems, take risks, reach out for assistance, think and feel about yourself, are major parts of your personality armor. These factors help determine your strengths and limitations. To further your understanding of yourself, examine these factors:

1. How Do You Handle New Challenges? When presented with a problem or challenge, do you become obsessed with the situation and spend time worrying about the outcome? Most often it is not the situation that's got you down. Rather, it's what you're thinking about the situation that's put you in a negative spin.

Obsessing and worrying about problems wastes valuable energy. Tunnel thinking, which is a result of this unproductive activity, can lead to anxiety. Anxiety is a fear of the unknown, and generally adds more anxious thinking to the situation. This thinking creates confusion and fear, often leading to debilitating and unproductive behavior. Reinforce your armor with factual thinking. Get out of the emotional center and raise yourself to a conscious level of thinking. Stay in the here-and-now. Don't allow your mind to wander to the "What if…" dimension. Stay with the facts to maintain control.

2. How Do You Manage Anger? If you suppress anger, you set yourself up for tough times. Unresolved anger leads to resentments, and resentments disable or destroy effectiveness. Reacting with anger is emotionally driven. It often leads to more anger. Learn to handle anger by responding to situations. Present the facts and make decisions based on this knowledge. If you're emotionally charged, you're reacting, not responding. You've let go of factual thinking and replaced it with uncontrolled verbal ranting or acting out behavior.

3. How Do You Face Problems? If you're reacting to a problem, likely you're using escape behaviors to deal with the situation. Rather than face it, you elect to procrastinate, deny, avoid, or simply hide from an encounter. Other escape behaviors might be eating, smoking, drinking, sleeping or compulsive behavior that provides temporary relief. To take control over this reactionary behavior, recognize that you're under stress and that these temporary acts do nothing more than make the existing problem worse. Raise your level of awareness to conscious thinking by asking, "What can I do right now?" Select from the options available to find productive substitutes for facing the problem. If you're worried about covering all the bills this month, is spending five dollars on cigarettes or a six pack really helping to solve the problem? Find rational and productive options to deal with problems.

4. Are You A Risk-Taker? This may be a double-edged sword. On the one hand, it may be wise to chance a new direction. On the other, caution may be the best defense. A general rule is to consider some middle ground, and not to get caught up in either extreme. When in doubt, raise your level of awareness by asking a question. For example, "What am I getting ready to do?" This puts you in at a focused level and in a better position to choose from your options.

5. Do You Seek Assistance? If you're a person who's walled off and self-protective, seeking assistance, even when it's best for you will be difficult. A mindset that thinks to seek help from others is to show a weakness, is indeed a weakness. A wise person knows when it's prudent to seek input from others, and does so.

6. How Are You At Maintaining a Positive Self-Esteem? This is your best self-control and self-image building process. Using positive self-talk can enhance your problem solving abilities. Instead of pulling yourself down with "I can't" talk, encourage yourself with what you can do.

Try these four process steps to Flip the Coin:

- A. Recognize the Negative Side. "I can't seem to do anything right."

- B. Look at the Flip Side. "I can do many things right. At the time, I'm making a mistake acting this way. What do I need to adjust?"

- C. Ask the Question: "Which of the two sides do I want to pursue?" "Which will be most productive for me now?"

- D. Always remember: The choice is yours to make.

Take little steps that provide you with incentives to continue being productive. Eliminate the urge to use escape behaviors—the easy way out behaviors. Support yourself with the self-talk statement "I'm O.K."

Tough times are one of the realities of life. They'll be with you, on and off, for the rest of your natural life. You can cope with them

Action Step #2: Self-Image: Effectively Using Strengths and Limitations 35

because you can outlast them. Check your personality armor. Stand guard at the doorway of your mind. Strengthen your weaknesses and enhance your strengths. You're worth the effort.

Productive Vs. Unproductive Emotional Habits

You're a creature of your emotional habits. Some of these habits carry you forward and can help produce outstanding results. For example, being motivated to set goals and succeed at a project brings about feelings of joy and accomplishment.

On the unproductive side, crippling emotional habits that get their introductions early in life include guilt, rejection, low self-esteem, feelings of inferiority, and depression. These are emotional factors that focus on unhappiness and can create psychologically crippling effects.

The interesting aspect of emotional habits is that you have the ability to adjust and manage them. Many of these habits form early in life when you don't have as many options consciously available to you. Today, now that you have more awareness, knowledge and control, whether you select positive or negative emotional habits is a matter of choice. This is especially true if you are aware of the fact that you are using a negative emotional habit to deal with a challenge. What's important to remember is that it's an emotional habit, and as a habit, it can be adjusted or changed.

The first step to changing a negative emotional habit is to recognize it for what it is—a habit. Be aware that while negative is normal, it's not productive. Identify the habit and try to understand that it's in control and making you feel miserable. Do you want to stop feeling miserable? You can flip the coin. You can choose to go to the positive side. You can regain control and start handling the situation more productively.

Step two is to be aware of the patterns that continue to support your habit. With patterned behavior, you'll keep returning to the negative processing. Recognize the "I can't" pattern and convince yourself that this pattern can be broken. Immediately start to replace it with a positive response, the "I can" response. If you've taken this step, you've flipped the coin!

Remember, it's not genetic. The power of negative thinking is learned behavior. It can be unlearned and changed. You can create negative learning experiences and wallow in them. Or you can create positive learning experiences and succeed with them. You do have a choice.

Make Yourself Ready For Change.

Self-imposed limitations are your greatest enemy as you navigate toward new goals. You want to succeed, but thoughts of past efforts can weigh heavily on the side of doubt. If you're focusing on the difficulties and uncertainties of the past, STOP! Remember, the past is what's happened to you, your experience. Flip the Coin. You're more likely to engage logical and rational thinking to appraise and manage the situation.

It's from these experiences that you can create new efforts. Evaluate results of your activities and determine their productivity. It's up to you to decide whether or not your future will be directed by your past. Use this simple evaluation system.

- **If the effort or activity was productive, keep adding to it.**
- **If the effort was unproductive, STOP. Do something else, anything else. Don't keep repeating the unproductive behavior.**

Your sense of direction is determined by your needs, expectations and goals. Taking control of this direction and the efforts exerted, will depend on you. Will you be willing to respond boldly and courageously in your actions? Or will you find yourself defensive and motivated only in terms of what others expect of you? Your understanding is determined by your ability to be honest with yourself. You need to be able to see and accept the truth, good or bad. Understanding is blocked when you react to misperception or faulty information. This is most notable if you fail to admit to errors, mistakes, shortcomings, or being wrong.

You're OK and you need to believe it. You'll have your share of difficulties, but these can be dealt with when you use the resources available from within. When you appreciate yourself for what you are, and treat others for their value and importance, you place importance on your abilities. Your efforts are directed toward seeing facts clearly, appreciating your self-worth, and improving your interactions with others.

Your abilities become your mission statement. Use them as your way of transporting your energies and self into a lifestyle filled with challenge and opportunity. Here are four guidelines to help define your mission:

1. Security: This represents your self-worth, your identity, your emotional anchorage, your self-esteem, your personal strength. It's basic to your survival. Understand that negative things will happen. When they do, step back, acknowledge their existence, tell yourself that you're OK, and ask the question: What can I do now? When you stay in the present and do what you can do, you establish your security and the foundation for future growth.

2. Guidance: Collect information that helps you to determine what's real or possible for you. Once you have this information and apply it to your needs and goals, you'll have the plan of action or direction for your productive movement.

3. Wisdom: This is represented by your perspective on life, your sense of balance, your understanding of how the various parts and principles apply and relate to each other. It's your judgment, discernment, and comprehension put into action. How you think directs your actions. Keep a positive focus, keep your head and hands in the same place, and you'll be expending productive energy.

4. Power: Here in lies your faculty or capacity to act, the strength and potency to accomplish something. This is your vital energy to make choices and decisions. You always have a choice in the actions or behaviors you exhibit. Learn to evaluate your actions. Ask the question: Is what I am doing right now productive? If yes, keep doing it. If no, stop and do something else.

Rely on what you have available to you. Stop merely wishing for things to change or get better. Take charge and make the adjustment and changes necessary for you to succeed and be happy. Place yourself in a position to make a difference. Understand your strengths and minimize your limitations. Allow the self-talk you use to reflect a positive and productive self-image.

Action Step #2: Self-Image: Effectively Using Strengths and Limitations 39

KEY LEARNING FACTOR #7
FLIP THE COIN

If you are dealing with a new direction, or a new idea, consider looking at both sides.

To do that, you can…

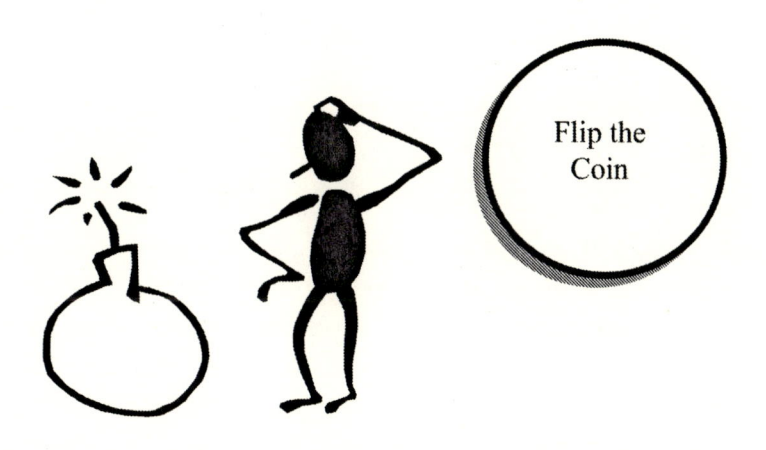

Flip the Coin

7

Action Step #3:
Accept Responsibility and Accountability For Your Actions and Behaviors

> *"You cannot strengthen the weak by weakening the strong. You cannot build character by taking away man's initiative. You cannot help men permanently by doing for them what they could and should do for themselves."*
>
> —*Abraham Lincoln*

Like a road under construction, self-mastery is a progressive state of improvement, not an end to be reached. You are the master of your own ship and have the ability to produce the results you most desire. If you decide, you can change your direction in life. Many people change their careers, sometimes by choice and other times because their jobs disappeared. In either case, perceptions of the event played a big part. Your perception is the truth as you see it, not necessarily as it is in reality.

Losing a job is a good example. Examples of corporate greed have created big holes in the lives of many people throughout the United States. People not only lost their jobs, but they also lost savings and retirement incomes that they were counting on for future security. For many the immediate reaction was devastation and panic. As time passes, it is interesting to note that some remain devastated, inactive, and depressed. Their perceptions likely are focused on the negative and they see a future with little hope or prosperity. Others have recovered, pulled themselves up and gone out and found new jobs. They are still hurting and may be in a weaker position, but they are starting to move forward. What's the difference between these two examples? Some might say attitude, and that is a big part of recovering or not recovering from a devastating blow. The message here is that you can either make things work for or against you. Whether you succeed or fail will be determined by what you choose to see and do with your situation and what's available to you. The roads you've already traveled, as well as those available to you, provide these resources and life experiences. To produce the results you want, you must be willing to take actions that will create your desired outcomes.

The Game of Life.

Each day presents new challenges. Regardless of your efforts, you're engaged in life's game that follows a pattern established since the dawn of man and recorded in Romans, Chapter 5: "Not only so, but we also rejoice in our sufferings, because we know that suffering produces endurance; endurance, character; and character, hope."

"But why is it that I have to suffer so much?" This is a universal statement, one whose content is interesting to examine. To begin with, suffering tends to present a negative focus and is seen as bad. In light of life's challenges, however, suffering is where your commitment to a new direction or activity starts. Suffering takes place as soon as you're moved out of your comfort zone and presented with new avenues to pursue.

Levels of suffering vary in their degrees of intensity. Light suffering requires minor adjustments to your normal routine. It is usually handled by putting forth a little extra effort. A request for you to work overtime might be such a suffering. It may interfere with some social or relaxation plans you had, but it does little to disturb your psychological or physical balance. Besides, the extra financial support generally eases the initial pain. Once beyond the initial reaction, you adjust and take on the task.

Moderate levels of suffering begin to shake your foundation a little. You recognize that you not only are being pushed out of your comfort zone, but are being challenged to search within yourself for resources that involve self-esteem and self-confidence. Questions emerge that test these factors—i.e., "Can I do this job?" "Is this a relationship that's going to be healthy for me?" "Will they accept me for this position?" Suffering at this level is internal. Perceptions begin to play a major role, and the battle is often with yourself rather than the situation at hand.

Heavy suffering takes its toll in the form of loss or perceived loss and extracts a great deal of your energy. The inability to accomplish a task to your satisfaction can present this level of loss. Criticism of your efforts, or lack of appreciation or acknowledgment for work completed, can create this depth of loss. You may experience a sense of failure, and focus on your thoughts and the impact your thinking generates. Here is where your thinking takes control and can create situations that don't even exist. Your thoughts rather than the actual event intensifies your suffering.

Are you noticing a trend? The fact is we often put way too much emphasis on our suffering. Understanding and processing this fact can lessen the impact. You always have options available to you. Look at the patterns you've established. Is your thinking filled with suffering when something takes a sudden turn?

Suffering leads to endurance. Once you leave your comfort zone and begin focusing on the task at hand, your level of commitment begins to take shape. Endurance is made up of about five percent ability and 95 percent "stickability." Your willingness to stick with your efforts enables you to determine your level of productivity. Finding your balance is important in this endurance factor. Watch your stress levels, as stress is productive to a point. Once it reaches the distress level, productivity goes down and emotional reactions go up. Understand yourself and recognize when you've hit the wall on distress. If this happens, take a break, back up and reevaluate the situation. Distress takes you out of control and depletes your energy very quickly.

Endurance leads to character. Character building emerges from the endurance exerted in a productive manner. With the proper focus on endurance, character development gains a positive and proper balance. This is truly the power within and the seat of self-mastery. When you believe in yourself, your character is emerging. You'll invest time and energy to develop yourself further. You are optimistic and constantly looking at what you can do. Your self-control is strong and this strength is exhibited in the way you achieve your goals.

So hope springs from the positive character emerging from the sustained suffering and endurance. Hope provides the incentive to continue to develop new opportunities. As long as there is hope, opportunities will abound. There always will be hope because there are always options. The only time an option will not be available is at the moment of death. Until that moment, hope remains alive. This then, starts the process all over again—new opportunities will take you out of your comfort zone, creating the element of suffering. Suffering leads to endurance. Endurance leads to character. That's the game of life!

Integrity is a Matter of Choice

Mistakes make major contributions to the learning process. There certainly are things you've done or events that have happened that you wish could be reversed. The past, however, doesn't change. The past is made up of those life experiences that allow you an opportunity to learn. Learning experiences will provide options and opportunities to progress to another level of development. Many of these learning opportunities bring reality to the saying, "The definition of a good learning experience is something that you wish was happening to someone else!"

Integrity emerges from these experiences with life events. It doesn't matter if you're young or old. You've already learned a lot about life. Wherever you find yourself on the scale of life, you have a lot more to learn about yourself and about the responsibilities you have to others. Integrity is built on your unwillingness to give in to easy outs offered when the more difficult choices of life present themselves.

Truth supplies the building blocks for your integrity foundation. If you've been lost in a sea of deception, truth will help you find yourself. Evaluate the breaks in your life. Check yourself before you ever compromise your integrity by taking the easier road. Once you turn your integrity over to a compromised position, you will never completely recover. It weakens the foundation and leaves you susceptible to future failings that could take you down even further. Keep this foundation. Work constantly to keep it shored up, steady, and stable.

Maintaining and enhancing your integrity position is a matter of choice. To maximize your position and continue to build on positive effort, a few how-to ideas might be helpful.

1. First and foremost, motivation is internal. It doesn't come from others. Other people can set the conditions for you to be motivated, but you must decide the level of motivation you'll exhibit. Some people are motivated to do nothing, and they do it well. You must decide to take control of your motivation and implement the number one force, determination. Determination will keep you in the hunt and help you reach your goals.

2. Get yourself emotionally ready. Whatever problem or challenge stands in your way, it is not going away on its own. You have to take control and manage the situation. To manage means that you have to do what it takes to put yourself in a position where you can continue to grow, develop, and progress in your environment. Watch your emotional reactions. They are usually out of control and irrational behaviors. Catch them quickly and refocus. That's the best way to regain

control of the situation, as opposed to letting the situation control you.

3. Develop a plan to manage your challenge. First, decide what needs to be changed or adjusted. What do you want to accomplish? Take stock of the situation. Does it require you to deal with an object (your job), a person (a relationship), or task (completing your tax return)? Think in terms of adjustments that can be made. Adjustments are smaller steps that allow for successes, and provide incentives to continue working toward a goal. The incentives derived from adjustments stimulate more productivity and eventual goal attainment.

4. Make your decision to change, and stick with it. You'll encounter old habits. Don't let past escape behaviors (procrastination, rationalization, denial) come into play when stress increases. The boredom becomes difficult, or "what ifs" of anxiety start to interplay. Assess your weaknesses, surround them with strengths, and take action steps to manage them.

5. Plan, organize, and commit to your new path. Be realistic with your changes. Collect the facts surrounding your decision, and develop a direction for achievement. Design productive plans and avoid making dramatic changes. All habits have a strong attraction point. Raise your awareness by figuring out what these contributing factors are and how to manage them. Watch for impulses to throw in the towel. These impulses come from the emotional center and are reactive. Hang in there. Change is difficult in the beginning. As you make adjustments, things start to get easier. As adjustments turn into successes, you'll realize and relish the benefits of your efforts.

Life will throw you your share of curves. Ward off deception or confusion and don't let them rein. If you take a strike, be ready, you still have two more coming. If you strike out, remember that the game's not over. Continue to give your best, put your character to work, and always maintain your integrity throughout the process.

What Could've Been is What is.

When you sit and think about what could happen if you'd done this or that, you're dreaming. This is a way to project your wants or desires, and can be useful in goal setting efforts. On the other hand, if you think about what you should've done with some past event, you're reflecting on an issue that you have no control over. What you could've been, in reality, is what you are right now. Don't lose sight of this fact. If you continue to reflect on the past, regrets fester and negative influences direct your behavior. To change your current situation, you must start with where you are right now. Avoid letting the past be an anchor, or your excuse.

Excuses are reasons for not doing or being able to do something. The first sign of an excuse pattern is the "I can't" response. "I can't change jobs, I've been doing this type of work all my life." "I can't get over the loss of this relationship,...he/she was my whole life." "I can't change now, I'm too old." The list goes on. The most important fact to remember about an excuse is that it's a "one time reason." In other words, you can use the reason once. After that you are aware of the limitations this fact presents, let it be. Once you know the fact being presented is an excuse, let yourself know that you have factual information on this issue, and now you can move on to something else. It's time to change your behavior or actions. You know if the direction you're pursuing is not working. That being the case, stop and do something different. Don't keep repeating the same "I can't" behavior pattern.

When you say you can't do something, understand that this is good information and move ahead. To keep reflecting on the can't issues is to waste time and energy. Once you know that you can't do something, simply ask, "What **can** I do?" Start doing what you can do no matter how simple or complex it might be. By doing what you can do, you move into a level of activity that can lead you to productive behavior.

KEY LEARNING FACTOR #8

The Game of Life

- You are a creature of habit.

- Habits are acts performed frequently during normal activities, and are functions of your subconscious mind.

- When performing habits, you are less likely to think about what you are doing.

- You develop standard patterns of response that reduce the amount of thought required for actions.

- You may act out an established behavior even when it no longer is the most effective response.

- You can change a habit and establish new ones.

- A habit starts with a conscious choice—you are in control of the decisions and choices you make.

- You can consciously choose to be negative, condition and reinforce that choice, repeat it often enough to be a habit.

- Habits are associated with reducing stress levels and increasing a sense of control.

We all have established patterns. With this in mind, think about this life skills building process:

- Opportunity leads to suffering.
- Suffering leads to endurance.

- **Endurance leads to character.**
- **Character helps build integrity.**

Maintaining and enhancing your integrity is a matter of choice.

8

Action Step #4: Understand And Appreciate Your Talents And Commit to Their Maximum Use

"We come into this world crying while all around us are smiling. May we so live that we go out of this world smiling while everyone around us is weeping."

—*English proverb*

Do Not Fear Criticism, Embrace It

Life is full of twists and turns. Hardly a day goes by when something new presents itself and you are required to make a choice as to how you will deal with this problem, task, or opportunity. Your choice is called a coping response. In some cases the response might be to do nothing and let the situation remain as it is. Another response might be to get upset, while a third might be to take hold and manage the situation. Regardless, deciding what to do will depend on the type of problem and its degree of difficulty.

When something does go wrong, the degree of difficulty tends to increase making the need to select a positive coping strategy more immediate. To ensure that this process will be successful, you must be able to determine how the situation or problem is impacting your self-image and how effective you are at creating new options.

When pushed, courage is one of the positive factors that can emerge. Courage is acting with fear, not avoiding it. Courage is you daring to be you. As much as you might resist revealing yourself to others, you must do so. You need other people in order to live life successfully. You need their respect, their support, and their goodwill. Don't let fear of criticism step in and become your enemy.

When accepting or receiving criticism, think about these four steps:

1. **Listen to the Feedback.** Try your best not to personalize the feedback. Don't get caught up with the person giving the feedback or the emotions that person may be expressing. Monitor your own feelings and try to keep them in control. As you listen to the feedback, try to separate it by keeping it factual (what is going on). Avoid getting emotional and reacting to it.

2. **Search for the Value.** Analyze what's being said. Make every effort to stay focused on the facts. This will help you manage inappropriate mannerisms of the presenter. Pay attention to the feedback. If something is repeated, it's probably important, at least to the presenter. Look for the importance it might have for you. Value can be derived and improvement can be made even when feedback is deemed to be unfair. Seize the opportunity to improve. Ask for specific behavior observations if the feedback isn't clear. By avoiding emotional reactions, you'll be able to turn a potentially negative situation into a positive developmental process for yourself.

3. **Do a Personal Assessment.** Focus on the facts. Keep your emotions under control. Respond, don't react, to the situation. Search to understand clearly what's being said. Do all of these things and you are in a position to make a decision. You can decide if the feedback is appropriate and whether or not you want to make the suggested adjustments. Look at these

awareness questions: Have you heard these criticisms before? Is the person who's providing the feedback a reliable source? Is that person making a valuable and needed observation? Is this person simply venting anger or frustration at you?

4. ***Voice Your Appreciation.*** Let the person know that you appreciate the feedback. You don't have to like the feedback or even agree with it, but future interactions with this person will be more productive if you control the situation and end it on a positive note.

Just as learning to take criticism is important, so is learning to give it. As stated earlier, you will need other people throughout life. Part of being successful with these people will depend on your capability to receive information accurately and your ability to give criticism appropriately. Here are six steps that might be useful to you.

1. ***Adjust Only What Can be Adjusted.*** If it can't be adjusted, then don't say anything about the situation. Avoid getting upset and criticizing what another person is unable to change. To criticize efforts or activities that cannot be adjusted will only create hurt feelings. Learning to manage your impulses when the urge is to tell someone off is an example of keeping yourself in the intellectual center instead of the emotional center. This helps you to remain in a controlled, productive place with the other person, as well as yourself. For example, you're working with a friend and he makes a mistake that is going to cost you both time and money. Rather than put him down for making the mistake, let him know that you're disappointed, but that the two of you can recover by doing what you can to make the situation better. By focusing away from the mistake, you take the situation to a higher level and to a place where productivity is possible. Both of you will benefit, and your chances of righting the wrong will be greatly increased.

2. ***Look for the Readiness Factor.*** Check your personal feelings and mood. Remember that anger generally breeds more anger. Also, no one appreciates or likes to hear criticism or negatives in the presence of others. Look for signs of readiness in individuals you are confronting. Are they in a safe place? A place where the message can be received without embarrassment, defensiveness or resentment? Are they ready to listen, or are they in an emotional state that does not allow for good communication? Picking up on these readiness factors will improve your ability to communicate with others.

3. ***Be Supportive.*** Use praise to open your feedback whenever it is possible. Be realistic with the praise. Don't use false praise that will be beaten down easily by your following comments.

4. ***Be Clear and Direct.*** Don't provide information of a critical nature unless you can be specific with your observations. Report the behaviors that you see, not your perceptions of those behaviors. Stay away from comments based on what you think you see. Get to the point and be specific.

5. ***Maintain Self-Esteem.*** When you believe you're pointing out a behavior that can be adjusted, do everything you can to help the person believe the adjustment can be made. Encouragement and support through the correction or adjustment effort will boost the individual's self-esteem.

6. ***Recognize Improvement.*** When you see improvement, no matter how slight, point it out. Incentive is the soul of success. Recognition of improvement will speed up the adjustment process. When you balance corrective feedback with recognition for improvement, you'll establish yourself as a person whose input will be valued as sincere and welcomed.

Fear of criticism can lead to worry, and worry to anxiety. Anxiety can produce symptoms that can ruin your day or generate a great deal of discomfort. Whether you suffer mild discomfort or psychological and physical incapacitation will depend on you. Knowledge is the first step to making fear a friend, and helping to harness anxiety into a productive ally. Through maintaining your dignity and courage, you'll not only learn to survive, you can overcome adversity and prevail.

Self-Confidence Foundation Builders

Self-confidence is a skill that has its roots in your early learning experiences. Your foundation for self-confidence is based on your perceptions of how you were accepted or rejected by your parents, friends, peers, and other perceived significant others. By focusing on this foundation, you can attain a more complete understanding of your current actions.

Four responses to life events can be closely associated with self-confidence. These four responses are major contributors to the foundation of self-confidence.

1. <u>Autonomy</u>. The poet Henley wrote, "I am the master of my fate, I am the captain of my soul." Autonomy allows you to be the master of your fate, and the commander of your soul. This power comes to you primarily because you have control over your thoughts. The foundation of autonomy gives you the ability to make choices. You can maintain control if you allow yourself to take the options available, and not depend on or blame others for the choices you make in life. It's easy to project blame when things go wrong. If you're still blaming your parents for where you are today, or complaining because the boss or friends keep imposing limits, you're not exercising your autonomy. You're not taking responsibility for your actions. You have the choice to make a place for yourself, no matter how many difficulties you have to overcome. You can decide where to turn, what to do, and how to get started when you take command of your fate.

2. <u>Connectedness</u>. This is a process skill. It requires you to make the choices necessary to develop strong, positive relationships at home, work, and in the community. Finding people whom you can support and who, in turn, can provide support is essential for being able to connect and form deep levels of attachment. To connect productively takes time. You were born with your relatives, but you pick your friends. Use the process wisely, and as you evaluate remember this bit of wisdom: Connectedness can be evaluated as "a ship big enough to carry two in fair weather, but only one in foul." (Ambrose Bierce). If you're connected, those with whom you are connected stand with you and will be pulling with you as though you were one.

3. <u>Perspective</u>. This foundation builder has to do with your meaning in life. What direction are you pursuing? What purposes have you placed on your efforts? What passion do you possess to pursue your goals? Failure is common in this area because you'll run into roadblocks that present temporary defeats. You may not realize that the temporary defeat is not a permanent failure. It does mean that new plans, new directions, or new opportunities need to be pursued. Evaluate your perspective on life. Consider the words of Napoleon Hill: "No man is whipped, until he quits—in his own mind."

4. <u>Tone</u>. The last foundation builder is tone. It relates to your energy level and your physical well being. We're all subjected to the negative influences of others. Tone will help you build a wall of immunity against these influences. To build this wall and to maintain a protective tone, you must recognize that you're susceptible to being lazy and indifferent to your weaknesses at times. Since negative influences tend to work through your subconscious mind (the part of the mind that doesn't distinguish between what's true or false), you must establish habits that will allow you to battle these influences. Your ability to

be able to perform under stress is dependent on your energy level. This ability is maintained by a continuous process of taking care of yourself e.g., regular exercise program, well-balanced nutritional program, acceptance of personal strengths and weaknesses, and being able to close your mind to people who try to negatively influence you in any way.

Here are seven steps for establishing positive self-confidence:

1. <u>Do your homework</u>. Learn everything you need to know to maintain your foundation builders. Knowledge is power. Generate facts, be careful of information that is based on opinion and myth.

2. <u>Develop your own style</u>. Know what you enjoy and what you're comfortable with in your environment. Trying to copy the style of others, or constantly trying to please others negates your personal effectiveness. Understand your strengths and limitations.

3. <u>Put your emotional life in order</u>. Avoid emotional crises that occupy most of your attention and energy. Remember to always "do what you can do." If you are blaming, ranting, raving, you're operating out of the emotional center and the situation or event is in control. If you're responding with factual statements or high levels of awareness, you're in the intellectual center and are likely in control or headed in that direction.

4. <u>Know your weaknesses</u>. When things don't go well, learn to do an appropriate assessment. If something does not work, then try something else. Don't keep repeating actions or behaviors that are unproductive. Take the things that work and build on them. Eliminate or stop using the things that don't work.

5. <u>Know your strengths</u>. Know what you're good at and the things you enjoy doing. Your strengths are your allies. Focus on them especially in difficult or trying times.

6. <u>Do away with your "I can't" attitude</u>. Replace it with a positive "I can if I think I can" attitude. Also remember the slogan, "As you think, so you go." Your actions and behaviors are directed by what you're thinking. Results are obtained from your actions and behaviors. Positive thinking raises your level of awareness to be more focused. This in turn encourages more enthusiastic and energy rich actions and behaviors, and leads one toward productive results.

7. <u>Develop a success-oriented network of friends and peers</u>. Pick the right people and trust them. Don't gossip. Remain loyal to your mentors.

From Will-be Achiever to Achiever Status

Most of us are Will-Be Achievers—people who work, assume responsibilities, and handle our own affairs. Yet, unfortunately, many of us find ourselves caught in systems we dislike. Often these systems look on and treat us as passive children—trainable at best, incompetent at worst. We find our intelligence insulted and give in to practices that limit our values of self-determination and self-control.

If this description fits, *Think* about these words from Abraham Lincoln: "You cannot strengthen the weak by weakening the strong. You cannot build character by taking away man's initiative. You cannot help men permanently by doing for them what they could and should do for themselves."

If you allow others to control your competency, responsibility, and productivity, they will define, direct and evaluate your usefulness to society according to their expectations, not yours.

As a "Will-Be Achiever" you have self-confidence. You're most familiar with the work you do, the skills you possess, and the demands of the work. You're in a position to manage yourself successfully. Why not take the step to *Achiever Level?* Here you find professional autonomy, responsibility and accountability, suitable rewards for your efforts, and an environment conducive for optimal performance.

Achievers are thinkers. They use their ability to think, enjoy doing so, and are paid for their efforts. One major reason for their success is the fact that Achievers are able to act. They take positive action on their work efforts. Instead of getting caught up in the fragmentation and fuzziness of immediate problems, they accept the challenge. Brainstorming new ideas, pulling things together, and filling in the details helps them to manage and work towards a productive outcome.

Elevate yourself from the Will-Be Achiever to Achiever level. Take time to learn about yourself. Identify the blocks that are currently preventing you from obtaining the status you desire from your work environment. Learn more about strengths and abilities that will allow you to master new job skills. Identify work behaviors that will enhance your ability to attain a sense of autonomy and job satisfaction. Lastly, align with others who provide a healthy, competitive spirit of cooperation and support.

Raise yourself to the Achiever level so that you can experience interesting, challenging work and the opportunity to further develop, expand, and maintain your career direction.

Action Step #4: Understand And Appreciate Your Talents And Commit to Their Maximum Use

KEY LEARNING FACTOR #9

The Foundations of Self-Confidence Building

AUTONOMY	=	**CONTROL AND CHOICE**
CONNECTEDNESS	=	**RELATIONSHIPS**
PERSPECTIVE	=	**DIRECTION AND OPPORTUNITY**
TONE	=	**ENERGY LEVEL AND PHYSICAL WELL-BEING**

Self-Confidence Building Through Conflict Management

- **IDENTIFY THE CONCERN** — WHAT IS DISTRESSING ME?
- **APPRAISE AND DEVELOP COMMITMENT** — WHAT AM I WILLING TO DO?
- **BECOME MORE AWARE OF BEHAVIOR PATTERNS** — HOW AM I HANDLING IT NOW?
- **DEVELOP AN ACTION PLAN** — WHAT AM I GOING TO DO?
- **TRY OUT THE PLAN** — HAVE I PUT PLAN IN ACTION?
- **EVALUATE THE PLAN** — WHAT RESULTS AM I GETTING?

9

Action Step #5: Deal with Reality and Manage Uncertainty

> "Take away my people, but leave my factories, and soon grass will grow on the factory floors. Take away my factories, but leave my people, and soon we will have a new and better factory."
>
> —*Andrew Carnegie*

Seeking Help

Seeking help in a situation that merits new information or direction is a positive element for success and forward progress. Although seeking help is a necessary and common process, it's one that's met with resistance and stubborn reluctance. Why is it so difficult for people to take this step? The answer lies in the instinctive behavior patterns established by the individuals involved.

You need help, but because of your stubborn determination to do it on your own, you keep plowing into the problem. Your determination is that of a bulldog that has grabbed hold of the old sock and would rather have its teeth pulled out as opposed to giving up the sock. Stubborn determination is an asset. However, you have to be able to assess the worth of the sock! Remember that a strength overused can become a weakness. It might be that new input could help evaluate the worth of hanging on to old ideas. With new input, you might be able to gain insights that are currently obscured by stubborn determination.

How do you get help? Ask for it. Another block in the old instinctive behavior process is the sense that asking for help is a sign of weakness. What's important to remember here is that without new information or facts you'll rely on old, perhaps already used, and possibly unreliable information. If new directions aren't created, you'll continue to travel down roads that have already led to dead ends. Stop and ask for help. This is the way to get the new directions necessary to continue productive advancement.

Help comes to you through the knowledge and wisdom of others who aren't as close to the problem, or who have insights because they've been where you are and have created new alternatives. So if you're resisting help because you see it as a weakness, get over it. Reach out, get new information and move beyond your unproductive stubbornness.

Exercise: Identify the need to reach out to another person. Take a situation and think about how you're managing it. Rate your management techniques as they apply to the following scale:

Co-operative: Agreement, harmony of feelings, ideas, and aims.
        (Very Low Risk)

Creative: Exploring and bringing into existence new ideas or direction.
        (Low Risk)

Conscious: Being aware of and consciously using mental faculties.
        (Low Risk)

Sensitive: Receptive and responsive to perceptions and impressions.
        (Moderate Risk)

Automatic: Learned behaviors operating out of the subconscious; subconscious does not determine right or wrong, good or bad.
(Moderate Risk)

Uneasy: Something is not right. Not sure what it is. Uncomfortable.
(High Risk)

Unaware: Totally out of touch with what is happening. In a state of denial.
(High Risk)

Anxious: Fear of the unknown. A major energy drain. Thought bombardment and confusion.
(Very High Risk)

If you find that you're operating in the "Uneasy," "Unaware," or "Anxious" categories, then you could use outside help. You're likely blocked and operating with old coping behaviors that are not working for you. Recognizing the "Uneasy" and "Unaware" categories is a good time to seek the help of a friend, spouse, or significant other. If you've reached the "Anxious" category, you might want to consider getting help from a trained individual—a minister, counselor, or psychologist.

Take charge by reaching out to others who can provide new information and insights. It's as easy as asking questions. There's no such thing as a dumb question. Be aware when those internal voices start replaying old, unproductive, self-reliant tapes. Seek help and expand your database of coping behaviors. By doing so you'll be putting yourself in a control position. It will expand your productivity and put you in a better place to cope with the changes that are creating challenges and conflicts in your life. If you find yourself in a bind, no matter how difficult or intense, give yourself a break. Seek Help!

Mask of Indifference.

Indifference is a human response to difficulties we encounter. Most of us have a difficult time understanding our feelings about certain situations or events. When these feelings arise, and we don't understand exactly what's happening, a mask of indifference is employed to allow for self-protection.

The mask of indifference that you wear is accurately described as your attempt to deny caring. Something goes wrong in your life and the immediate comment is "I don't care." A valued relationship is about to break up and your comment might sound like this: "If that's the way it is, that's the way it's got to be." Hate is often described as the opposite of love. Not true, because to love or hate someone you must be actively involved with them. Love and hate are emotions of affection, one positive and one negative. The opposite of both love and hate is indifference, the active denial of caring and the most destructive of all.

Wearing a mask of indifference is normal, human behavior. Although it's normal, it's not productive. Learn to stand guard at the doorway to your mind. This will help you to recognize some of the behaviors that may be motivated by unproductive patterns. Corrective action is needed to deal effectively with these patterns.

Consider the following **Model of Indifference** and see where you fit in the situation described.

You have been confronted by a new situation or issue at work. You can choose one of two directions of pursuit. First off, you can react and engage your emotional center. This allows you to become upset and likely take actions that are totally irrational. In this state blame becomes a convenient escape or outlet. Perhaps past experiences of ranting and raving have gotten you through similar situations. The emotional center does not stop you from engaging in these behaviors because rational thought does not enter the picture. This is an automatic reaction based on habitual or experienced behavior patterns. It is likely that the results to be achieved are going to be unproductive, and might even lead to more conflict related to the event or past events. The escalating effects of this conflict are occurring because a pattern that you tend to use habitually is failing to yield any productive results. The likely outcome might even lead you to a concluding reaction of "I don't care, I'm not going to give in on this one." This is a sign of indifference.

Consider this level of indifference and how it might logically proceed through the following model:

Indifference feeds *strife.*

Strife leads to *confusion.*

Confusion leads to *turmoil.*

Turmoil leads to *rebellion.*

Once you proceed from indifference to strife, you are getting off track and likely moving deeper into the emotional center. Problem solving becomes more difficult because you get offended (*strife* level), and try to set the record straight (*confusion* level). Continued levels of confusion causes you to react with anger (*turmoil* level). The receiver of your anger is very likely to return anger. You are headed into the *rebellion* level. You prepare for battle as chaos starts to rein. The irony of this whole thing is that you more than likely are not even sure why it has taken this route. If common sense doesn't prevail, and often it doesn't, resentment is the characteristic outcome. Resentment is like a cancer. It grows until it destroys all forms of logic and rational pursuits.

Look at your second option. Once the situation hits, stop and back up. Think about being flat up against a wall. If you found yourself in this position, with your head buried face first against the wall, what would you see when you opened your eyes? That's right, wall! At times you can get so close to the challenge that you fail to see the options that might be available. With your face flat up against the wall, you have severely limited your options. Back up. Take three steps back. Now what do you see? You see wall, but more of it. Looking around you might see a window, a door. Depending on what it is you want to accomplish, you have opened up the possibility of options. You are now in a much better position to choose more productive actions. Before this point, it appeared that your only option was to keep pushing.

As you backed away from the wall, you were starting to put yourself in a position to pursue other avenues for coping with your challenge. If you find yourself in a disagreement, step back and ask yourself a question. For example, you might ask "what can I do right now?" This takes you out of the emotional center and raises you to a level of processing that is more rational. This is called the Intellectual Center, a place where problem solving becomes a realistic avenue of pursuit. Since the intellectual center allows for exploration of factual information, you can disagree with an opinion or thought, but you do so respectfully and with conscious logic. Remember, you're away from the wall. You can survey the options before you, and proceed in rational and logical form to manage the challenge. This approach allows you to work with your habitual behavior, adjust unproductive behaviors, and make adjustments to allow you to move to a more productive level. This puts you in a position to deal with the changes you might be encountering. It helps you become a **maker** and **maintainer** of change. It allows you to leave the rebellion level without compromising yourself, your values, or your desires for successful outcomes.

This scenario can be summarized by looking at behavior change. If you want to move from negative behavior posturing to more positive behavior outcomes, identify where you might be in this behavior change sequence:

>Strife leads to confusion.

>Confusion leads to turmoil.

>Turmoil leads to rebellion.

>Rebellion can create a situation enmeshed with false pride.

False pride can be controlled and abated by humility.

Humility helps develop integrity.

Integrity leads to honor.

Honor allows you and others to gain from the change.

You can learn to respond to any event by raising your level of awareness. To do this, ask the question: "What is it about this new issue or challenge that bothers me?" By asking this question, you have raised yourself to a conscious level and placed yourself in a position to focus on the facts surrounding the challenge. You are in a place where you can begin to select options that will allow you to find more productive outlets, and set you up to successfully manage challenges that must be confronted.

Not Knowing Can Hurt You

"What you don't know can hurt you." This is true if you're experiencing stress, or even distress, in your daily life. Whenever stress mounts, the negative voices get louder. As you sit and ponder what's happening, the negatives become consuming and much energy is wasted in the self-talk that debates the issues. "I can't seem to do anything right anymore." "If only I hadn't made that investment." "Why do others seem to have all the luck?" Listen to yourself. Isn't it pathetic! Having a pity party accomplishes nothing.

Maybe it's time to stand up and count your assets. If you're not pleased with where you are today, take inventory and get to know yourself better. "That's great," you say, "But how?" Start by finding a way to defeat the negative inner voices that are so compelling and controlling. One way to blunt them is to develop accurate facts about yourself.

To open yourself to other possibilities or alternatives is a risk-taking venture. Immediately, old thoughts enter and the self doubt begins: "But what if…" "I'm just not sure…" "This is going to be pretty hard and…" Add to these thoughts your best friend's or colleague's comments: "You can't do…" "You're too young (or old) to do that now." It's interesting how these comments often reflect the status of the person delivering them. Don't let the thoughts or reasons of others become the limiting factor for your efforts. Provide yourself with accurate information regarding strengths and limitations and then start motivating yourself toward success. A friend recently gave me this very sound and positive advice: "Assume nothing, and try everything."

Change: An Ending With a New Begnning

Change, although a certainty of life, is difficult at best for most of us to endure. Even though it can offer many benefits, it often presents with frightening moments of uncertainty. This fellow's experience illustrates this point.

> After eating his mother's cooking for 21-years, consisting of deep fat frying and highly seasoned foods, a week of eating his new wife's cooking cured something he had never known, a life long case of heartburn. Concerned by this change, rather than feeling relief, he rushes into the hospital emergency room, clutching his stomach and yelling: "Doc! Doc!! Help me! I'm dying. My fire went out!"

Although you may have lived with a painful situation for a long time, there comes a time for giving up the past and moving on. Don't waste time hating the past no matter how bad it was or how much suffering you experienced. You have no control over your past. The only benefit that can be derived is to learn from the past and let the experience enable you to change and to move in the direction that is best for you now. In some cases, enduring difficult, painful situations may have been necessary in order for you to believe that change was needed. Self-destructive attitudes often take a lot of discouragement before there is a willingness to give them up. Some people believe that they will be rescued by a divine intervention and are still waiting for this miracle to occur. You've reached a level of maturity when you accept the idea that you are the agent of your own change and growth.

Time spent suffering in past experiences is not wasted time if it provides a direction or plan of action. Many hopeless relationships continue until one of the people reaches a point where change becomes the option. This time comes for some when it is felt that the children are old enough to accept and endure a separation or divorce. For others it might be when a new love reaffirms the fact that they are lovable. Still others might suffer until they no longer feel guilty about leaving a relationship.

Change needs personal validation. You must be willing to admit and understand mistakes in order to feel right about making a change. A common pattern is to see a person rushing from one unhappy relationship right into another that is almost identical in its debilitating effects. This is not change. This is a person operating in the emotional center, attempting to prove in an irrational and illogical manner that the decision to leave the first relationship was a correct one.

Change begins when you can leave the emotional center. You can achieve this task by asking the question, "What can I do right now?" When you ask this question, you elevate yourself to the intellectual center, raise your thinking level from an automatic base to that of consciousness, and ready yourself to start thinking of possible options for change. Change occurs when you seek a higher level of self-honesty. Learning to accept yourself as you are, recognizing your strengths and limitations, and planning new directions to meet your own expectations, allows you to put into motion the actions and behaviors that help you find your way.

Change involves transition. This is a natural process of disorientation and reorientation that marks a turning point on the pathway to change. Situational transitions such as death, divorce, loss of a job, loss of a relationship, tend to have three benchmark commonalties. They are:

1. ***An ending.***

2. ***A period of confusion and distress.***
3. ***A new beginning.***

The Ending. Letting go is difficult. It is frightening because you discover parts of your past still have a hold on you. This becomes evident as you display bouts of self-doubt, centered on your inability or lack of control to survive the change. These episodes of doubt create challenges and emotional reactions that are confusing to you and to others around you. Ending are often difficult to discuss because they are surrounded by feeling of regret and shame. These feelings emerge because you are sad, disappointed, or angry at what has happened to you. You don't believe you deserve to be in the position you are in, and because of your emotional responses may be demonstrating irrational or illogical behaviors. In reality, what you had before may not have been that good. Hanging on to the past you stunt your ability to rationally deal with the ending. You find it difficult to discuss your true feelings because of the emotional reactions that block rational understanding. Lastly, you might be experiencing confusion and embarrassment because you were unable to manage an ordinary life situation successfully. This may be compounded by the fact that you think others are managing situations like this easily.

Endings are difficult. Everyone finds them difficult. Because of this fact, don't slide into the emotional center. It is irrational to think that this is only happening to you and that you are the only one who has a problem. Deal with the ending through the intellectual center. Separate fact from fiction. Deal with the facts as best you can. Keep them in the here-and-now. Establish a direction and plan of action that is based on your needs, goals and expectations. By doing so, you will be setting into motion a logical and realistic problem-solving guide.

Period of Confusion and Distress. This is a time when you will feel lost and empty. It is a very unproductive time-out, characterized by inattentive activity and ritualized routine. You can better endure the consequences of this phase by keeping these points in mind:

1. Your emptiness is a natural result of the ending process.
2. This can be an opportunity to lay the groundwork for a new life.
3. By realizing how common this experience is, you will feel less alone.
4. Developing new tools for the road ahead will help you confidently face the future.

How does one develop these tools? Basic to the entire process is a sense of surrender. Initially give in to the emptiness and stop struggling to escape. Find a regular time and place to be alone. Keep a written journal of your experiences and thoughts when you are in the "time-out" zone. Think through the questions: "What moods am I going through?" "What am I thinking about, without realizing that I am in that thought?" "What decision do I wish I could make?" "What dreams do I remember dreaming?" Take this opportunity to sort through these things and start establishing your new direction. "What are your needs?" "What are your expectations?" "What are your goals?" Remember that in change the limiting circumstances are part of what ends. You are no longer held back from doing those things you want to do, especially if the past was one of the factors holding you down. Think of what you would miss if your life ended today. What dreams, what convictions, what talents, what ideas, what qualities would go unrealized? Set your expectations in motion through your plans and directions.

A New Beginning. New beginnings are available to you. You likely will have trouble with the newness involved. You may wish to start your new beginning, but some part of you resists doing so. The fear of making a major mistake (self-doubt) still pervades your thought processes. Anxieties and confusion arise from the fear that real change destroys the old ways. The old ways might still provide a sense of security, false as it may be. To make a successful beginning, you must understand what it is within you that undermines your resolve and casts the shadows of doubt on your plans and actions. In developing this understanding, pay attention to what is real regarding your new beginning, and what is a defensive reaction to the past ending.

Taking action can be done when you direct your thinking to the options available to you. There are several things you can do to create your new beginning.

1. Stop getting ready. **Act!**

2. Begin to identify yourself within the final results of the new beginning.

3. Take one step at a time, explore change, look for the benefits.

4. Diffuse your purpose from goal to the process of reaching your goal.

5. Take your time. Take care of yourself in small ways.

6. Arrange temporary structures and develop true systems of support.

7. Don't act for the sake of action. Be aware of emotional center activities.

8. Recognize when you are uncomfortable and work with these feelings.

9. Recognize the characteristic pattern of change: things end, there is a period of emptiness, and then things begin anew.

KEY LEARNING FACTOR #10

MODEL OF INDIFFERENCE

- A new situation arises.

- It challenges a habitual behavior pattern you tend to use consistently.

- Your reaction: "I don't care, I'm not going to change."

- This is an example of INDIFFERENCE.

- Consider the following MODEL OF INDIFFERENCE:

    - INDIFFERENCE feeds STRIFE.
    - STRIFE leads to CONFUSION.
    - CONFUSION leads to TURMOIL.
    - TURMOIL leads to REBELLION.

HABITUAL BEHAVIOR REACTION TO INDIFFERENCE

- Once you get into STRIFE, you are starting to get off track, and likely moving into the EMOTIONAL CENTER.

- You get offended (STRIFE Level), you try to set the record straight (CONFUSION Level), and likely react with ANGER (TURMOIL Level).

- The receiver of your anger most likely returns anger. You are headed into the REBELLION Level. All Hell is about to break loose!! You are prepared for battle—and likely are not even sure WHY!

TURNING A NEGATIVE INTO A POSITIVE:

- Back up. If you disagree with a change, do so respectfully and from the **INTELLECTUAL CENTER**.

- Remember a HABIT is a Learned Behavior (You have learned how to be offended).

- Be the one to break this pattern. LEARN to make allowances.

- Become a MAKER and MAINTAINER of change.

10

Action Step #6:
Understand and Commit To Your Choices and Options

> *"Too many men drift lazily into any job, suited or unsuited for them; and when they don't get along well they blame everybody and everything but themselves. Grouches are nearly always pinheads, small men who have never made any effort to improve their mental capacity."*
>
> —**Thomas Edison**

Life is a continuum. You may be experiencing times filled with hopes and dreams, trials and tribulations, joy and happiness, and/or dread and sadness. Because you could be experiencing either positives or negatives described in the previous sentence, Self-Mastery is a tool that can provide you with the guidance necessary for productive development.

Doubt is a Creator of Indecision.

Doubt is generated when information needed to pursue a particular thought or direction is incomplete. The more doubt that you experience, the less decisive you become. Therefore, doubt becomes the creator of your indecision. If you're not careful, it can cause a paralysis so debilitating that anything requiring your action becomes a major challenge.

"Doubt is generated when information needed to pursue a particular thought or direction is incomplete." Examine this statement please. If you're having difficulty making decisions in your life, you may be close to mastering your problem. Is it as simple as needing more accurate information to help you reach a conclusion? If so, recognize this fact, collect new information, and get to work on implementing a new problem-solving process. Search for enough information to start putting together a plan of action or develop a direction you might want to take.

To make any headway with doubt, you must first recognize that you're in control of your behavior and you can do anything with it that you choose to do. A simple emphasis change and you're in the process of eliminating doubt. As you think, so you go. You're now in a position to receive information. New information that's necessary to help you understand why you're behaving the way you are. Your new direction is motivated by assessing what it is that you're trying to do, what you're aiming for, and what your intentions are. Keep in mind that just asking these questions alone will not suffice. You cannot be expected to know all of the answers. Don't let doubt become your enemy. Search for new information.

Constructive Coping

You face daily challenges in the areas of biological and social growth, career and work development, and family involvement. To cope constructively with each of these areas, you must have an understanding of how they interact within your daily life patterns. You cope on a daily basis, but what does it mean to cope constructively?

To cope constructively means to confront challenges and develop responses that adequately deal with these challenges in such a way that you continue to grow and develop. This is a process of confronting tasks and developing responses that result from successive life experiences. Your key to successful constructive coping is to identify what your life choices are and what they involve. Once identified, your goal is to act as rationally as you can in exercising these choices. The process can be outlined in four steps.

Step 1. <u>Identify what the problem or challenge is</u>. Think through the situation and search for a better understanding of what's causing the stress. To accomplish this task, follow these guidelines:

a. Determine the origin and possible interaction of the situations. For example, if something unanticipated happens, ask: "What's going on?" "Where's the problem coming from?" "What's the origin of the stress?" "Is the source of the problem in one area or is it the result of an interaction among several areas (e.g., work vs. family vs. social commitments)?"

b. Determine the difficulty of the challenge. Coping is more difficult if several life areas are involved. If this is the case, you're more likely to be overloaded or conflicted to the point where any constructive coping may be impossible. A major question to ask is "Which life area is the primary source of the problem and how are other life areas interacting to create or enhance the problem?"

Step 2. <u>Diagnose yourself</u>. Attempt to improve understanding of your resources, feelings, and needs as they apply to the situation. Most people are good at identifying external sources of stress, but fail miserably at assessing their responses, or at identifying realistic ways to cope given their strengths and limitations. A practical guide for achieving self-insight is to ask these questions when confronting a challenge:

a. What feelings is this challenge arousing in you: anger, frustration, despair, relief, anxiety, etc.

b. If your feelings are preventing you from solving the problem, do you have a choice about those feelings? Can you get past your anger, anxiety, fear, etc. to gain control and act on the problem? If not, the problem is within you. What can you do about that?

c. Are you contributing to the problem by the way you're reacting or responding to the situation? Can you change your response to improve the situation?

d. How have you responded in the past to similar experiences? Did your response have a desirable or undesirable outcome?

The most difficult part about diagnosing yourself is to be aware of what you're feeling and to determine what triggers those feelings. Feelings based on subconscious forces need more work to understand and control.

Step 3. <u>Select a coping response</u>. Based on your diagnosis of the problem and yourself, decide how you need to deal with the stressful situation. A coping response can be anything you choose to do in order to deal with the challenge at hand. You can choose to do nothing, or you can act constructively about the problem. Innovative efforts that may help include: rethinking the situation, redefining your role, focusing on your strengths, and applying coping responses that have worked in the past.

Step 4. <u>Diagnose the effects of your coping responses</u>. Evaluate whether your efforts have achieved their purpose. Has the challenge been confronted and met, and the problem managed? Finding a process that works for you can boost your productivity.

Constructive coping is an on going process. Find ways to cope which will help you bypass the tendency to blame others for failures you're experiencing. Utilize the ideas, perspective, and emotional support of others in order to grow and develop. Establishing meaningful relationships with others can be one of the most important skills you can develop to aid you in your constructive coping efforts.

Exercise: Write down a situation that is likely to occur and create distress for you. List the conditions that might be associated with that situation (e.g., people present, location, time of day, etc.). After making this list, think of the behaviors that this condition might bring out in you (e.g., make me angry, frustrate me, make me laugh, cause me to want to leave, makes me stop and think, etc.). After creating your two lists, go back through the conditions. On a scale of 0 (No control) to 100 (Total Control), determine how much control you have over each condition. Now do the same for your behaviors. What is it that you discovered from this exercise? Likely you're now aware that you have very little control over most conditions, but that you've got a great deal of control over your behaviors. If you find yourself in a situation causing distress, think about the behavior you're exhibiting and ask, "What can I do right now?" Remember, you can control your behavior. That will help you deal with the situation more effectively.

Action Step #6: Understand and Commit To Your Choices and Options 79

KEY LEARNING FACTOR #11

Managing Conflict: An Assessment Model

THE STEPS:

1. **Situation/Event creates a conflict.**

2. **You move to Frustration, and then on to Anger.**

3. **At Anger, you either Respond or React.**

4. **Reacting leads to a lack of control—the situation controls you.**

5. **Responding leads to Management—you start to manage the situation.**

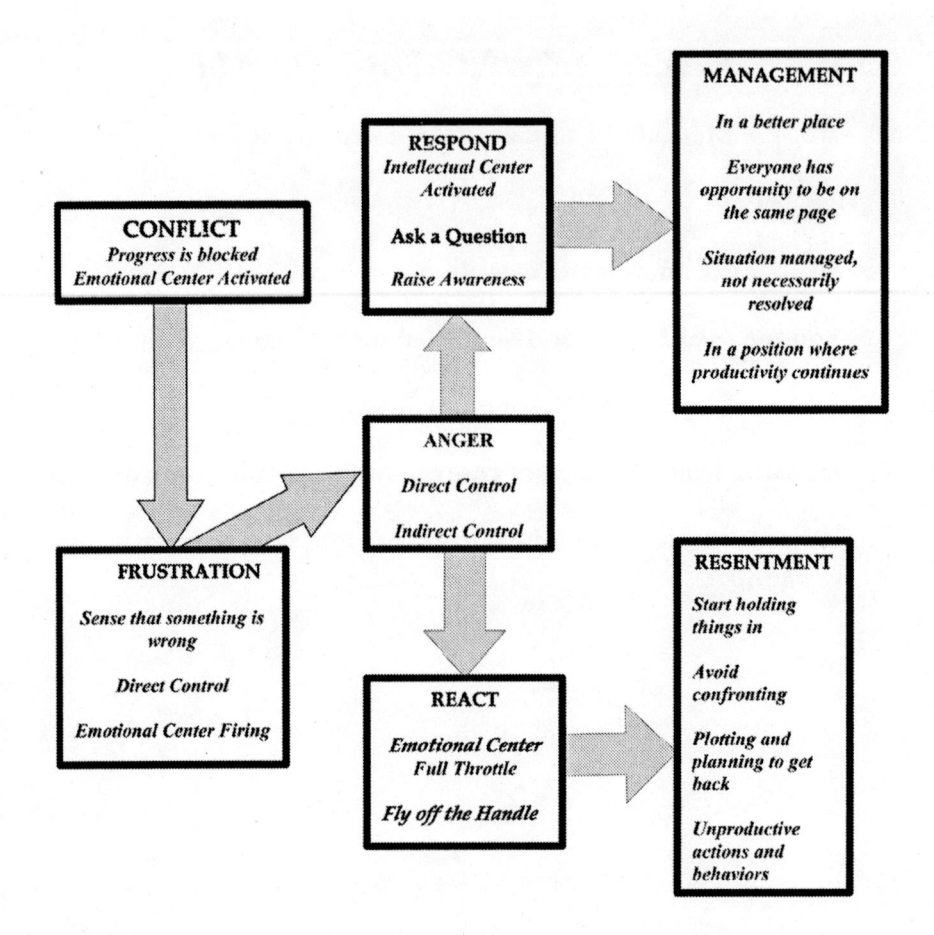

Self Coaching Your Self-Mastery Road Map

CONFLICT
Progress is blocked
Emotional Center Activated

RESPOND
Intellectual Center Activated
Ask a Question
Raise Awareness

MANAGEMENT
In a better place

Everyone has opportunity to be on the same page

Situation managed, not necessarily resolved

In a position where productivity continues

ANGER
Direct Control
Indirect Control

FRUSTRATION
Sense that something is wrong
Direct Control
Emotional Center Firing

REACT
Emotional Center Full Throttle
Fly off the Handle

RESENTMENT
Start holding things in

Avoid confronting

Plotting and planning to get back

Unproductive actions and behaviors

11

Conclusion: Your New Beginning

o o o o o o o o o o o o o o o o o o o o o o o o o o o o o
"Cherish your visions and your dreams as they are the children of your soul; the blueprints of your ultimate achievements."

—*Napoleon Hill*

Self Mastery will give you your keys and your road map. Now you're ready to begin. How? By taking hold of the steering wheel, managing the accelerator and brake, navigating onto the roadway and maneuvering down the road. There'll be potential obstacles. There may even be unknown danger ahead: bridges out, roads closed, incompetent drivers, car problems, just to name a few. But that's all right, because you're determined to reach your destination.

Not only that, you're ready for the unexpected because you're in control and can remain in a productive position. You know that to remain calm and to manage the situations that arise is the best way for you to succeed. You also know that if you get lost or confused, all you need to do is slow down, or even stop, and collect more information. You know that to be lost is not the worst thing that can happen. The worst thing that can happen is not to even attempt to reach the destination you believed was real or possible. Know your commitment and follow your plan. You'll be successful and the outcomes will be rewarding and satisfying.

Above all, the foundation of success will be your integrity. It's the true "seed for achievement" and is based on your honesty and truth. Integrity starts with knowing yourself and possessing a true understanding of your abilities, talents and goals. Being truthful with yourself means taking the responsibility to make the best use of what you have available to you. You have your mind, your abilities, your talents, and your time. You take them with you wherever you go and no one can take them away from you. They truly represent your wealth.

Invest your wealth in your will to succeed. Place yourself above the competition by being creative. Be true to yourself as you follow the law of cause and effect. Never give less than your best. Remember that you have time, time which cannot be saved, stopped, or held back for even a second. Make full use of your riches. It's never too late.

Conclusion: Your New Beginning   83

KEY LEARNING FACTOR #12

KEEP YOUR HEAD AND HANDS

IN THE SAME PLACE

**by doing so
YOUR RISK OF MAKING MISTAKES
GOES DOWN!**

APPENDIX A

Affirmation Thoughts to Live By

"Remember, you're OK!"

"Stop the negative. Make a positive statement."

"Your thinking guides your actions and behaviors."

"Become conscious of the actions that are not producing the results you desire."

"Select options that make adjustments to obtain the desired results."

"As you think, so you go."

"Positive thinking produces positive actions."

"Negative is normal, it's just not productive."

"You can demonstrate positive behavior if you're generating positive thoughts."

"Keep a good handle on your awareness issues."

"You're right now exactly what you want to be."

"It's not the situation that gets you down, it's what you think about the situation that does you in."

Ask the question, "What can I do right now?" to take you out of the emotional center and put you into the intellectual center.

"You're a creature of your emotional habits."

"If an effort is unproductive, STOP. Do something else, anything else."

"Your understanding is determined by your ability to be honest with yourself and to see and accept the truth, good or bad."

"Your sense of direction is determined by your expectations and goals."

"Your abilities become your mission statement. Never give less than your best."

"Keep a positive focus and you'll be expending productive energy."

Evaluate your actions. Ask the question: "Is what I'm doing right now productive?" If yes, keep doing it. If no, stop and do something else.

"To produce the results you want, you must be willing to take actions that will create your desired outcomes."

"Suffering leads to endurance. Endurance leads to character."

"If you've been lost in a sea of deception, truth will help you find yourself."

"To manage a situation is to do what you have to do to put yourself in position where you can continue to grow, develop, and progress in your environment."

"Assess your weaknesses and take steps to manage them."

"Excuses are reasons for not doing or being able to do something."

"Courage is acting with fear, not avoiding it."

"Seize the opportunity to improve."

"Knowledge is the first step to making fear a friend, and helping to harness anxiety into a productive ally."

"A strength overused can become a weakness."

"Learn to stand guard at the doorway to your mind."

"Learn to become your own best friend."

"Integrity starts with knowing yourself and possessing a true understanding of your abilities, talents and goals."

"Integrity is built on your unwillingness to give in to easy outs offered when the more difficult choices of life present themselves."

APPENDIX B
Recommended Reading List

Aguilera, Donna C., and Janice M. Messick. *Crisis Intervention Theory and Methodology*. Saint Louis: The C.V. Mosby Co., 1974.

Alessandra, Anthony J., and Phillip L. Hunsaker. *The Art of Managing People*. New York: Simon and Schuster Inc., 1980.

Bach, Richard. *Illusions—The Adventures of a Reluctant Messiah*. New York: Dell Publishing Co., 1981.

Bates, Marilyn, and David Kiersey. *Please Understand Me, Character and Temperament Types*. Del Mar: Prometheus Nemesis Book Co., 1984.

Benjamin, Alfred. *The Helping Interview, Third Edition*. Boston: Houghton Mifflin Co., 1981.

Burns, David D. *The Feeling Good Handbook*. New York: Penguin Books, 1989.

Carnegie, Dale. *How to Stop Worrying and Start Living*. New York: Simon and Schuster, Inc. 1948.

Cousins, Norman. *Human Options*. New York: W. W. Norton and Company, 1981.

Covey, Stephen R. *The Seven Habits of Highly Effective People*. New York: Simon & Schuster, 1989.

Covey, Stephen R., Merrill, A. Roger, Merrill, Rebecca A. *First Things First*. New York: Simon & Schuster, 1994.

Ellis, Albert, and Robert A. Harper. *A New Guide to Rational Living*. North Hollywood: Wilshire Book Company, 1975.

Fromm, Erich. *Man For Himself*. Greenwich: Fawcett Publications, Inc., 1947.

Helmstetter, Shad. *Choices*. New York: Pocket Books, 1989.

Hill, Napoleon. *The Master-Key To Riches*. New York: Fawcett Crest, 1965.

Maltz, Maxwell. *Psycho-Cybernetics*. New York: Essandess Special Editions, 1960.

Mandino, Og. *A Better Way to Live*. New York: Bantam Books, 1990.

Mandino, Og. *The Greatest Miracle In The World*. New York: Bantam Books, 1975.

Mandino, Og. *The Greatest Salesman In The World*. New York: Bantam Books, 1968.

Mandino, Og. *The Greatest Salesman In The World Part II, The End of the Story*. New York: Bantam Books, 1988.

Mandino, Og. *The Return of the Ragpicker*. New York: Bantam Books, 1992.

Peale, Norman Vincent. *The Power of Positive Thinking*. New York: Fawcett Crest, 1956.

Robbins, Anthony. *Awaken the Giant Within*. New York: Simon & Schuster, 1991.

Rohm, Ph.D., Robert. *Positive Personality Profiles*. Atlanta: Personality Insights, 1997.

About the Authors

**Michael S. Haro, Ph.D.
and
Michael S. Haro, II, B.A.**

Michael S. Haro, Ph.D., founder of the Center for Change Management, is a management consultant based out of Houston, Texas. The focus of the Center is to provide cost-effective consulting and training aimed at improving individual and organizational productivity through increased awareness, assessment and action of how individuals and organizations respond to change and stress.

Dr. Haro has bachelor's and master's degrees from Ball State University and his doctorate from Kent State University. He is a licensed psychologist. Dr. Haro conducts numerous onsite and public seminars dealing with change readiness, stress management, and leadership development.

Michael S. Haro, II, B.A., is Vice President of the Center for Change Management. He is an honors graduate of St. Lawrence University, Canton, New York. Currently, Mr. Haro is an elementary school teacher in the Fort Worth Independent School District, Fort Worth, Texas.

About the Center for Change Management

The Center for Change Management is led by its founder and President, Michael S. Haro, Ph.D. The focus of the Center is to provide cost effective consulting and training aimed at improving individual and organizational productivity through increased awareness, assessment and action.

Dr. Haro received his Bachelor's and Master's degrees from Ball State University and his Ph.D. from Kent State University. He is a licensed psychologist. He is a former college professor at a major university and currently consults with industry, public and health care organizations. Dr. Haro has done extensive work with ADSI, NASA, Entergy, Texas Petrochemicals, Jacobs Engineering and various schools and professional organizations.

Dr. Haro specializes in the areas of employee development, team building, training, individual assessment, counseling, interviewing and self coaching. He offers seminars and training dealing with Self Coaching, Change Readiness, Stress Management and Personal Assessment.

The *MSH PROFILE*, a proprietary tool used in selected training modules, individual assessments, and available for licensing, was developed by Dr. Haro in 1994. It is designed to help individuals develop a better understanding and awareness of themselves and their behavior patterns. Taking less than two minutes to complete, the profile stimulates participants' thinking to more effectively manage change and stress in their lives. The MSH PROFILE can provide the knowledge to help participants avoid unproductive situations in the first place, and stop wasting time and energy on what doesn't work for them.

To receive more information on Training Programs or the MSH Profile Report, write or call The Center for Change Management.

The Center for Change Management
16414 Havenhurst Drive
Houston, TX 77059
Telephone: (281) 488-5460
Fax: (281) 488-1300
e-mail: msharo@ix.netcom.com

0-595-65305-7

Printed in the United States
1369000001B/278